Top 25 locator map
(continues on inside
back cover)

◄───

KU-156-821

CityPack
Berlin

**CHRISTOPHER AND
MELANIE RICE**

Christopher Rice writes
regularly on Eastern Europe
and Russia and holds a
PhD from the Centre for
Russian and East European
Studies at Birmingham
University. His wife, Melanie,
is also a writer and shares
his fascination with this
part of the world. The
Rices have written a
number of guidebooks
including *Berlin* in the
AA/Thomas Cook series.

AA Publishing
Find out more about AA Publishing and
the wide range of services the AA provides
by visiting our web site at *www.theAA.com*

Contents

life *5–12*

Introducing Berlin *6–7*

Berlin in Figures *8*

Contemporary Berliners *9*

A Chronology *10–11*

People & Events
  from History *12*

how to organise your time *13–22*

Itineraries *14–15*

Walks *16–17*

Evening Strolls *18*

Organised Sightseeing *19*

Excursions *20–21*

What's On *22*

top 25 sights *23–48*

1 Sanssouci *24*

2 Cecilienhof *25*

3 Klein-Glienicke *26*

4 Spandau Zitadelle *27*

5 Jagdschloss Grunewald *28*

6 Sachsenhausen *29*

7 Ethnologisches Museum *30*

8 Schloss Charlottenburg *31*

9 Kurfürstendamm *32*

10 Kaiser-Wilhelm-
  Gedächtniskirche *33*

11 Bauhaus-Archiv *34*

12 Kulturforum *35*

13 Kunstgewerbemuseum *36*

14 Tiergarten *37*

15 Topographie des Terrors *38*

16 Brandenburger Tor *39*

17 Checkpoint Charlie *40*

18 Gendarmenmarkt *41*

19 Unter den Linden *42*

20 Museumsinsel *43*

21 Pergamon Museum *44*

22 Berliner Dom *45*

23 Nikolaiviertel *46*

24 Alexanderplatz *47*

25 Schloss Köpenick *48*

Index *94–95*

● About this book *4*

best *49–60*

Museums *50–51*
Galleries *52*
Places of Worship *53*
Bridges *54*
Political Sights *55*

Parks & Gardens *56*
Views *57*
Statues & Monuments *58*
For Children *59*
What's Free *60*

where to... *61–86*

EAT

German Restaurants *62–63*
Other European
    Restaurants *64–65*
International Restaurants *66*
Middle Eastern, Turkish &
    Out-of-Town Restaurants *67*
Cafés *68–69*

SHOP

Department Stores &
    Souvenirs *70*
Boutiques & Designer Clothes *71*
Second-hand & Offbeat *72*
Galleries *73*

Antiques, Glass & Porcelain *74*
Markets & Food Shops *75*
The Best of the Rest *76–77*

BE ENTERTAINED

Theatres & Concerts *78*
Cabaret *79*
Pubs, Bars & Clubs *80–81*
Folk, Jazz & Rock *82*
Sport *83*

STAY

Luxury Hotels *84*
Mid-Range Hotels *85*
Budget Accommodation *86*

travel facts *87–93*

Arriving & Departing *88*
Essential Facts *89–90*
Public Transport *90–91*

Media & Communications *91–92*
Emergencies *92*
Language *93*

Credits, Acknowledgments and Titles in this Series *96*

About this book

KEY TO SYMBOLS

✚ Grid reference to the accompanying fold-out map, and Top 25 locator map

✉ Address

☎ Telephone number

🕐 Opening times

🍴 Restaurant or café on premises or near by

Ⓤ Nearest underground (tube) station

🚆 Nearest railway station

🚌 Nearest bus route

⛴ Nearest riverboat or ferry stop

♿ Facilities for visitors with disabilities

✋ Admission charge

↔ Other nearby places of interest

❓ Tours, lectures or special events

► Indicates the page where you will find a fuller description

ℹ Tourist information

Citypack Berlin is divided into six sections to cover the six most important aspects of your visit to Berlin. It includes:
- An overview of the city and its people
- Itineraries, walks and excursions
- The top 25 sights to visit
- What makes the city special
- Restaurants, hotels, shops and nightlife
- Practical information

In addition, easy-to-read side panels provide extra facts and snippets, highlights of places to visit and invaluable practical advice.

CROSS-REFERENCES
To help you make the most of your visit, cross-references, indicated by ► show you where to find additional information about a place or subject.

MAPS
The fold-out map in the wallet at the back of the book is a comprehensive street plan of Berlin. The first (or only) grid reference for each attraction refers to this map. For example, the Kunstgewerbemuseum (Museum of Applied Art), on Matthäikirchplatz, has the following information: ✚ G6 – indicating the grid square of the map in which the Kunstgewerbemuseum will be found.
The Top 25 locator maps found on the inside front and back covers of the book itself are for quick reference. They show the top 25 sights, described on pages 24–48, which are clearly plotted by number (**1** – **25**, not page number) from west to east across the city. The second grid reference for the Top 25 sights refers to this map.

ADMISSION CHARGES
An indication of the admission charge (for all attractions) is given by categorising the standard adult rate as follows:
✋ Expensive (over 5 euros; DM10), Moderate (2.5–4.5 euros; DM5–9), Inexpensive (under 2.5 euros; DM5).

BERLIN
life

Introducing Berlin *6–7*

Berlin in Figures *8*

Contemporary Berliners *9*

A Chronology *10–11*

People & Events from History *12*

Introducing Berlin

Chinese Teahouse in the park at Sanssouci

THE CITY'S HISTORY

Although nearly 900 years old, Berlin grew into a major capital city only after Prussia emerged as an important power in the 18th century. Industrialisation and imperial ambitions stimulated rapid expansion and prosperity during the 19th century that lasted until the outbreak of World War I in 1914. Disastrous defeat and subsequent abolition of the monarchy made Berlin a centre of political turmoil. This period of social and economic unrest, of cultural experiment and diversity, became internationally known as the Weimar years, named after the ill-starred republic that yielded to Hitler in 1933 in an attempt to restore order. The Allied victory over Nazi Germany led by Great Britain, the United States and the Soviet Union was soon followed by the Cold War between the West and communist Eastern Europe. The formal division of Germany left Berlin in a contentious position, prompting the Communists in 1961 to construct their notorious border wall through the centre of the city. The unification of Germany in 1990 has enabled Berlin to reclaim its status as the historical capital of Germany. With the arrival of federal president, chancellor and ministries, Berlin replaced as the seat of government Bonn, the city that served as provisional capital for 50 years. Business boomed and it sometimes seemed that Berlin was one vast construction site.

CITY FOR THE 21ST CENTURY

The transformation to model city is by now far advanced. To appreciate the fact, visit the rejuvenated parliament building, the former Reichstag, and take the elevator to the viewing gallery in the dome for a panoramic view of the metropolis-in-the-making. Locate Berlin's 'green lung,' Tiergarten park, and to the north the embryonic Regierungsviertel (Government Quarter), scheduled for completion in 2005. Cranes on the far side of the river mark the

Lehrter Bahnhof, a railway station on four levels, which by 2004 will form a major transport hub. In the opposite direction you'll make out the stunning new glass and brick towers of Potsdamer Platz, by day a shopping and business centre, after dark an entertainment venue. In the middle ground, flanked by banks and embassies, is the Brandenburg Gate, and Friedrichstrasse in the East, rebuilt almost from scratch and now a rival to the West's Kurfürstendamm with its shopping centres, offices and luxury hotels. Nearby is the site of Checkpoint Charlie, the famous border crossing point, today an architect's playground of businesses and shops.

Sculpture near Breitscheidplatz

COUNTRY IN THE CITY

One third of Berlin is green space and Berliners use it to full advantage. Every weekend they set out from the marinas at Wannsee for the placid waters of the Havel. Ornithologists bird-watch on the shores of the Müggelsee, dog-owners head for the Grunewald forest and hikers for the woodland around the Schorfheide. There are even beaches in this landlocked city. Tiergarten park, an oasis of rural tranquillity, is only a stone's throw from the heart of the city.

BERLINERS

Berliners are restless and energetic. Their chief characteristic, described by other Germans as *Berliner Schnauze* ('Berlin mouth'), implies both a taste for quick-fire humour and a tendency to show off. Most visitors find the people genial and easy-going: they wear their much-heralded industriousness lightly. Some friction remains between 'Ossis' (former East Berliners) and 'Wessis' as the former try to adjust to Western ways, while the latter sometimes resent competition for jobs and the fact that, for some time, they will need to subsidise their fellow citizens.

SEAT OF GOVERNMENT

A completely remodelled parliamentary district, scheduled for completion in 2005, will contain government ministries, press and information offices, embassies and the Federal Chancellery with a striking sculpture by Basque artist, Eduardo Chillida, symbolising German unity. Other buildings will be located in the old Government Quarter south of Unter den Linden. The 18th-century Schloss Bellevue will remain the official seat of the federal president.

7

Berlin in Figures

Population and growth
- The population of Berlin in 2000 was 3,500,000.
- 46 per cent is male; 54 per cent female; the only Berlin district with more men than women is Kreuzberg.
- 12 per cent of the population is foreign, of which more than one third are Turkish.
- 27 per cent is under 25; 14 per cent is over 65.
- Historical growth:
  1600 – 9,000 inhabitants
  1709 – 57,000
  1800 – 172,000
  1900 – 1,888,000
  1920 – 3,879,000.
- The municipal reform of 1920 made Greater Berlin the largest city on the European continent.

Environment
- Berlin's municipal area is 886sq km, an area 9 times greater than that of Paris.
- 24 per cent of Greater Berlin consists of rivers, lakes and forests; 10.9 per cent is recreational.
- The highest natural hill is Grosse Müggelberg (115m).
- Germany's northernmost vineyard is in Berlin's Kreuzberg.
- Berlin has 1,800,000 dwellings, 953 bridges, 5,102km of public streets and 196km of navigable waterways.
- Berlin has one of the most extensive public transport networks in Europe with 9 U-Bahn lines, 12 S-Bahn lines, 26 tram lines, 155 day bus lines and 56 night bus lines; more than 1 billion passengers use the system annually.

Leisure
- Each year there are more than 32,000,000 visits to Berlin's theatres, cinemas and palaces.
- Berlin has 3 opera houses, 150 theatres and concert halls, 200 fringe theatres, 50 children's theatres, 170 museums, 9 palaces, 274 libraries, 1,900 sports clubs, and 7,000 cafés, restaurants and pubs.

Contemporary Berliners

EBERHARD DIEPGEN

Born in Berlin in November 1941, the mayor of Berlin, Eberhard Diepgen, was educated at the Free University of (West) Berlin. While still a student, he joined the Christian Democrat Party and went on to chair the West Berlin party organisation. A member of the Berlin Chamber of

Eberhard Diepgen

Deputies from 1971 to 1981, he was also a deputy in the German Bundestag (Parliament). He was first elected Mayor of Berlin in 1984 and was in the happy position of presiding over the unification celebrations in 1990. Re-elected in 1991, 1995 and 1999, Diepgen has overseen the transfer of Government from Bonn, the official opening of the new Federal Parliament and the ongoing architectural transformation of the city.

CLAUS PEYMANN

New artistic director of the Berliner Ensemble theater, Claus Peymann (*b*1938) wants to put a forward-looking and dynamic stamp on this world-famous institution. Peymann made his reputation for controversial direction in Bochum and Stuttgart, staging new works by young rebels such as Peter Handke and Thomas Bernhard. From 1986 to 1999 Peymann was in charge of the prestigious Burgtheater in Vienna. The Berliner Ensemble was formed in 1949 by playwright Bertolt Brecht and his actress wife Helene Weigel. Peymann, one of Germany's best known directors, is now setting the Berliner Ensemble on an enterprising course, offering experimental opportunities to contemporary authors and possibly sidelining the Brecht heritage.

DIETRICH FISCHER-DIESKAU

Renowned German baritone Dietrich Fischer-Dieskau was born in Berlin in 1925 and began his singing career at the Berlin State Opera. Since then he has won numerous musical awards (more than one Grammy, for example), especially for his recordings. Best known throughout his career for his interpretation of German Lieder, he has also premiered works by Britten, Henze and others. He lives in Charlottenburg.

9

A Chronology

1244	First recorded mention of Berlin.
1369	Berlin becomes a member of the trading association known as the Hanseatic League.
1443	Frederick II of Brandenburg builds the first Berlin castle (Schloss).
1448	Berliners defend their privileges in the revolt known as 'Berliner Unwille.'
1618–1648	Berlin is devastated by Austrian and Swedish armies during the Thirty Years' War and the population is halved to less than 6,000.
1701	Elector Frederick III proclaims himself King Frederick I of Prussia.
1740	Accession of Frederick the Great.
1806	Napoleon enters Berlin.
1847	Werner Siemens and Johann Georg Halske manufacture the first telegraph in a house on Schöneberger Strasse.
1848	Germany's 'bourgeois revolution'; demands for greater middle-class representation in government; workers take to the barricades.
1871	Berlin becomes the capital of a united German Empire under Kaiser Wilhelm I and the Prime Minister of Prussia, Prince Otto von Bismarck.
1881	The world's first electric tram goes into service in Berlin.
1918	After World War I, Kaiser Wilhelm II abdicates to make way for a German Republic.
1920s	Against a background of growing social and economic instability, Berlin becomes a cultural powerhouse and entertainment centre. Grosz, Einstein, Brecht, and Gropius all flourish.
1933	Adolf Hitler becomes Chancellor of Germany.

1936	Berlin plays host to the Olympic Games. Black American athlete Jesse Owens triumphs on the field.
1938	On Kristallnacht (the 'night of breaking glass') the Nazis orchestrate the destruction of Jewish property and synagogues.
1939–1945	World War II.
1945	Berlin lies in ruins, the population reduced from 4 million to 2.8 million. The city is divided into four zones of occupation, administered by French, British, US and Soviet forces.
1948–1949	An attempt by the Soviet government to force the Western Allies to withdraw from Berlin by blockading the city is foiled by a gigantic airlift of food, medicines, clothing and supplies.
1949	Germany is divided into the Federal Republic and the German Democratic Republic, leaving Berlin stranded in the communist GDR.
1953	Construction workers in East Berlin, protesting low wages, provoke a full-scale uprising, which is put down by Soviet tanks.
1961	The flood of East Germans to the West is staunched by the building of the Berlin Wall.
1963	John F. Kennedy demonstrates American support for West Berlin in his famous 'Ich bin ein Berliner' speech at Schöneberg Town Hall.
1989	On 9 November the collapse of communism in Eastern Europe leads to the opening of the Berlin Wall and its eventual demise. Only a few sections remain standing, one as a memorial.
1994	The last of the occupying Allied and Soviet forces formally withdraw from Berlin.
2000	Berlin once again becomes the capital of a united Germany.

11

People & Events from History

FREDERICK THE GREAT
The great Prussian monarch was a living contradiction who had a profound impact on the future of Berlin and of Germany. An enthusiast of the Enlightenment, with its emphasis on rationalism, tolerance and intellectual curiosity (Voltaire was a guest at the Prussian court), his first action on the European political stage was aggressive – the cynical exploitation of Austrian weakness by the invasion of Silesia.

NAPOLEON
When Napoleon ordered the occupation of Berlin in 1806 he did not realise that he was sowing the seeds of his own destruction. His actions served as a powerful stimulus to Prussian patriotism, galvanising politicians into making the military and institutional reforms that led to the historic defeat of the French at Leipzig in 1813. In strengthening the Prussian nation at the expense of Austria, Napoleon also unwittingly contributed to German unification.

ADOLF HITLER
An Austrian by birth and a Bavarian in sympathies, the German Führer regarded Berlin with undisguised distaste, partly because, as a hotbed of Communism and radical protest, it was the last bulwark of resistance to the Nazi regime. Berlin's place at the political heart of the regime singled it out for special attention from the Allies through the last months of World War II. By 1945 Hitler's boast that he would transform Berlin into a new world capital, Germania, had a hollow ring.

THE END OF THE WALL
For 40 years after the end of World War II Berlin was an island of Western democratic values in a sea of Communist totalitarianism. The building of the Berlin Wall in 1961, a knee-jerk response to the growing exodus of Berliners from East to West, brought ideological confrontation into even sharper focus. The opening of the Wall in November 1989 was consequently a deeply symbolic moment in modern European history.

Statue of Frederick the Great, Unter den Linden

BERLIN
how to organise your time

ITINERARIES *14–15*

The Ku'damm, Tiergarten
& Unter den Linden
Schloss Charlottenburg
& the Wannsee
Museumsinsel, Alexanderplatz
& the Nikolaiviertel
Sanssouci & Potsdam

WALKS *16–17*

Prenzlauer Berg
& the Scheunenviertel
Schöneberg

EVENING STROLLS *18*

**ORGANISED
SIGHTSEEING** *19*

EXCURSIONS *20–21*

Bernau
Lutherstadt Wittenberg
Lübbenau
Brandenburg

WHAT'S ON *22*

Itineraries

Berlin is so large, and offers such a wealth of places to visit, that planning your sightseeing can be a daunting prospect. These four one-day itineraries will help you cover some of the major sights in a practical way.

ITINERARY ONE	**THE KU'DAMM, TIERGARTEN & UNTER DEN LINDEN**
Morning	Stroll east along the Ku'damm (► 32) from Adenauerplatz U-Bahn station, for a morning of shopping and people-watching. Pause for coffee in Café Kranzler (► 68). Later, visit the Kaiser-Wilhelm-Gedächtniskirche (► 33) in Breitscheidplatz.
Lunch	Shop in the food hall of KaDeWe (► 70) and have a picnic in the Tiergarten (► 37).
Afternoon	Take bus 100 or 200 from Zoo Station or the Tiergarten to the Brandenburg Gate (► 39). Walk across Pariser Platz and along part of Unter den Linden, turning off to reach Französische Strasse U-Bahn station. Take the U-Bahn south to Kochstrasse and visit the Haus am Checkpoint Charlie museum (► 40).
ITINERARY TWO	**SCHLOSS CHARLOTTENBURG & THE WANNSEE**
Morning	Travel to Richard-Wagner-Platz U-Bahn station (or take bus 145 from Zoo Station) and visit the former royal palace, Schloss Charlottenburg, and its gardens (► 31). Cross Spandauer Damm to view the treasures of the Egyptian Museum (► 50) or the Berggruen Collection (► 52).
Lunch	Restaurant Eosander (► 69).
Afternoon	Take the S-Bahn (line 3) to Wannsee for an afternoon on the largest inland beach in Europe or go on one of the many possible boat trips. Bus 116 will take you to the Glienicker Bridge (► 26), bus 216 (A16) to the ferry (daily 8–8) for Pfaueninsel (Peacock Island ► 59).

ITINERARY THREE	**MUSEUMSINSEL, ALEXANDERPLATZ & THE NIKOLAIVIERTEL**
Morning	Take bus 100 or the U- or S-Bahn to Friedrichstrasse. Cross the footbridge from Am Kupfergraben to reach Museumsinsel (Museums Island), and spend the morning in the Pergamon Museum (➤ 44).
Lunch	The terrace of the popular Operncafé and restaurant (➤ 69) is near Museumsinsel.
Afternoon	Walk west along Unter den Linden (➤ 42) and turn left at the statue of Frederick the Great into Bebelplatz. Cross Französische Strasse into Gendarmenmarkt (➤ 41).
	Walk to Stadtmitte U-Bahn station and travel to Alexanderplatz (➤ 47). Explore the scenic Nikolaiviertel (➤ 46) and its cafés.
ITINERARY FOUR	**SANSSOUCI & POTSDAM**
Morning	Travel to Potsdam Stadt S-Bahn station and take bus 612, 692 or 695 to Sanssouci (➤ 24). After visiting the Schloss, stroll through the grounds, perhaps lingering over a coffee at the Drachenhaus.
Lunch	Choose one of Potsdam's many cafés, perhaps the café-restaurant Am Stadttor (➤ 68).
Afternoon	Wander through Potsdam's charming old streets, such as Brandenburger Strasse, Am Neuen Markt and Dortustrasse. The Dutch Quarter (Holländisches Viertel), with its rows of red-brick, gabled houses, was built in the 18th century for construction workers labouring on the new town ordered by Frederick William II. Visit the Potsdam Film Museum in the Marstall (former royal stables) on Breite Strasse.
	Alternatively take bus 694 from just beyond the Nauener Tor to Schloss Cecilienhof (➤ 25), or take the train to Babelsberg for a tour of the famous studios (➤ 59).

15

Walks

THE SIGHTS

- Neue Synagoge (➤ 51, 53)
- Monbijou Park (➤ 59)
- Sophienkirche (➤ 53)
- Elisabethkirche
- Volkspark am Weinberg
- Water tower
- Käthe Kollwitz memorial

INFORMATION

Distance 5km
Time 2½ hours
Start point Oranienburger Strasse
➕ J4
🚇 S-Bahn Oranienburger Strasse
End point Husemannstrasse
➕ K2
🚇 U-Bahn Eberswalder Strasse
🍴 Café: Café Oren (➤ 68); Restaurant: Restauration 1900 (➤ 63)

Café on Husemannstrasse

PRENZLAUER BERG AND THE SCHEUNENVIERTEL

Walk eastwards along Oranienburger Strasse, heart of the Scheunenviertel (Barn Quarter), which became the Jewish Quarter in the late 17th century. Dominating the skyline is the golden dome of the Neue Synagoge (New Synagogue). Lower down, on the right, is Monbijou Park, once the grounds of a royal palace, and, on the left, the remains of the Old Jewish Cemetery, destroyed by the Nazis.

Turn left into Rosenthaler Strasse and then take the first left into Sophienstrasse. This neighbourhood is now an artists' enclave. Between Sophienstrasse and Oranienburger Strasse are the historic courtyards known as the Hackesche Höfe. These 19th-century workers' houses and factory workshops are now smart restaurants, boutiques, art galleries and theatres.

Continue along Sophienstrasse, passing the 18th-century Sophienkirche, then follow Grosse Hamburger Strasse. No. 11, 'The Missing House,' commemorates its occupants, who were all killed in an Allied bombing raid. Cross Kopperplatz into Ackerstrasse, the heart of an old working-class quarter.

On the opposite side of Invalidenstrasse are the remains of Schinkel's Elisabethkirche (1832). Walk east along Veteranenstrasse, past the Volkspark am Weinberg and join Kastanienallee briefly before turning right into Schwedter Strasse. Cross Senefelderplatz into Kollwitzstrasse. On the right, just off Belforter Strasse, is the 19th-century water tower used by the Nazis as a makeshift torture chamber in 1933. At Kollwitzplatz is a memorial to the Expressionist artist Käthe Kollwitz.

Husemannstrasse now has a lively café scene, but the refurbished tenements disguise a more squalid late 19th-century working-class life.

SCHÖNEBERG

First mentioned in 1264 as Sconenberch, the residential quarter of Berlin now known as Schöneberg was not formally incorporated into the city until 1920.

Before you leave Wittenbergplatz station, take time to admire its art-deco interior, then walk down Kleiststrasse to Nollendorfplatz, the centre of 1920s nightlife, and still home to the Metropol, dating from 1906 (formerly a theatre, now a nightclub). Walk south along Maassenstrasse, crossing Nollendorfstrasse. British author Christopher Isherwood, whose reminiscences of Berlin life in the 1930s inspired the film *Cabaret*, lived at Nollendorfstrasse 17. The next square you come to, Winterfeldtplatz, is best known for its twice-weekly market.

At the end of Maassenstrasse is Pallasstrasse; the Sportspalast that once stood here was the scene of many of Adolf Hitler's rallies. The flak tower nearby is a wartime survivor and was part of the city's defences.

Cross Pallasstrasse into Elssholzstrasse. On the left is Kleistpark, named after the German Romantic poet Heinrich von Kleist, who tragically shot himself on the shores of the Wannsee in 1811, aged only 34. Just inside the park is the former Supreme Court of Justice (Kammergericht), where Count von Stauffenberg and other instigators of the failed July Bomb Plot to assassinate Hitler were tried in 1944. Just a few months later the judge, the infamous Roland Freisler, was killed when the building sustained a direct hit during an Allied bombing raid.

Turn right into Grunewaldstrasse, then left into Martin-Luther-Strasse. Dominating John-F-Kennedy-Platz is the Rathaus Schöneberg, former town hall of West Berlin. It was from the balcony of this building that President John F Kennedy delivered his famous 'Ich bin ein Berliner' speech on 26 June 1963, only months before his assassination.

THE SIGHTS

- ● Wittenbergplatz U-Bahn (► 60)
- ● The Metropol
- ● Nollendorfstrasse 17
- ● Winterfeldtmarkt (► 75)
- ● Kleistpark
- ● Rathaus Schöneberg

INFORMATION

Distance 5km
Time 2½ hours
Start point Wittenbergplatz U-Bahn
🚻 F7
Ⓤ U-Bahn Wittenbergplatz
End point Rathaus Schöneberg
🚻 F9
Ⓤ U-Bahn Rathaus Schöneberg
🍴 Café: Tim's Canadian Deli (► 69)

Plaque commemorating Kennedy's speech

17

Evening Strolls

INFORMATION

Kreuzberg
Distance 2km
Time 1 hour
Start point Görlitzer Bahnhof
L7
U-Bahn Görlitzer Bahnhof
End point Kottbusser Strasse
L7
U-Bahn Kottbusser Tor

Savignyplatz
Distance 2km
Time 1 hour
Start point Savignyplatz
D6
S-Bahn Savignyplatz
End point Savignyplatz
D6
S-Bahn Savignyplatz

'STAGE IN THE WOODS'

Warm summer evenings are perfect for a visit to the Waldbühne, Berlin's most famous open-air stage. Completed in 1936 and rediscovered in the 1980s, the Waldbühne hosts everything from rock concerts to film shows (➤ 82).

KREUZBERG

Emerge from the shadows of Görlitzer Bahnhof into the uneven glare of a typical Kreuzberg junction. The litter-strewn pavements, spray-painted walls, and the sounds of the Orient are enlivened after dusk by a crazily vibrant night scene – pool halls, offbeat cafés, milk bars, all-night pubs and numerous inexpensive restaurants. Head northwest along Oranien-strasse to Heinrichplatz where you will find the welcoming café-bar Rote Harfe (➤ 81).

Further on, turn left onto Adalbertstrasse and head for Kottbusser Tor. The pungent odour of the kebabs and onions sold at numerous Imbiss stands fills the night air at 'Kotti.' There are more bars on Kottbusser Strasse, which leads down to the Landwehrkanal. See this night stroll as an appetiser. If you like the Kreuzberg flavour, come again and explore a little further afield: try Wiener Strasse, Dresdener Strasse, Manteuffelstrasse and Hasenheide.

SAVIGNYPLATZ

Berliners are notorious show-offs and un-ashamedly fond of enjoying themselves. You will find evidence of both these characteris-tics in the streets around Savignyplatz, which claims the city's highest concentration of café-bars and international restaurants. Cross the square into Carmerstrasse. At Steinplatz turn left into Goethestrasse, then left again into Grolmanstrasse to return to Savignyplatz.

Savignyplatz

The night zone extends south of Kantstrasse too, so walk west along Kant-strasse as far as Schlüterstrasse. Turn left, and left again onto Mommsenstrasse, then make your way back to Savignyplatz via Knesebeckstrasse.

Bring the evening to an agreeable end with a drink in the Schwarzes Café (➤ 69).

Organised Sightseeing

CITY TOURS

BERLIN CITY CIRCLE (BVB)

Two-hour city circle tours. Buy a half-day ticket if you want to hop on and off. English commentary on tape.

✉ Kurfürstendamm 225 ☎ 8859880

BEROLINA SIGHTSEEING

Bus tours of Berlin and Potsdam-Sanssouci with an English commentary on tape. Departures from the Ku'damm.

✉ Meinekestrasse 3 ☎ 88568030

SIGHTSEEING TOURS (STADTRUND-FAHRTEN)

Hop on – hop off city tours with an English commentary. Includes Schloss Charlottenburg and Prenzlauer Berg.

✉ Kurfürstendamm 231, or Unter den Linden 14
☎ 7524057

WALKS

INSIDER TOUR

English-speaking Berliners give visitors an insider's view of the city. This walk takes up to three hours.

✉ Boppstrasse 3 ☎ 6923149

THE ORIGINAL BERLIN WALKS

'Discover Berlin' and 'Infamous Third Reich Sights' are the two English-language tours.

✉ Harbigstrasse 26 ☎ 3019194

OUT–OF–TOWN EXCURSIONS

BBS (Berliner Bären Stadtrundfahrt)

Bus tours to Potsdam and the Spreewald with an English-speaking guide.

✉ Rankestrasse 35 ☎ 35195270

SEVERIN AND KÜHN

City tours and tours to Dresden, Potsdam and the Spreewald. English-speaking guide.

✉ Kurfürstendamm 216 ☎ 8804190

BERLIN BY BOAT

Reederei Heinz Riedel
For an original view of Berlin, the round-trip of canals and waterways offered by this steamboat company is hard to beat. Departures are from Kottbusser Brücke.

✉ Planufer 78
☎ 6934646

Stern und Kreisschiffahrt
Tours include the Havel, the city canals and the River Spree. Other destinations: Köpenick, Muggelsee and the Spreewald. Departure points: Tegel (Greenwich Prom.), Wannsee Station, Jannowitzbrücke and Treptower Harbor.

✉ Puschkinallee 15
☎ 5363600

Yacht Charter
Hire a 14m yacht with friends for a luxury cruise on the Havel.

✉ Berliner Strasse 26–7, Potsdam
☎ 8214658

BERLIN BY BUS 100

The route from Zoo Station to Alexanderplatz takes in many of Berlin's main attractions. Bus 100 runs via Siegessäule, the Reichstag and Brandenburger Tor, before continuing down Unter den Linden to Alexanderplatz. Departures fom Zoo Station every 10 minutes.

Excursions

BERNAU

Bernau is a fine example of the attractive old villages that surround Berlin. Founded in 1232, Bernau has preserved its medieval heritage to a surprising extent. The battlements and defences of the robust mile-long city wall are largely intact. Find out more about the town's past at the local history museum, a monument in its own right, in the 14th-century Steintor. Also of interest are the 16th-century former grammar school, the Marienkirche and the 18th-century hangman's house.

LUTHERSTADT WITTENBERG

Wittenberg is famous throughout the world as the cradle of the Reformation. It was here that an obscure monk named Martin Luther began a protest against the Roman Catholic Church that ended in his excommunication and the birth of Protestantism. The Lutherhaus, on Collegienstrasse in the former monastery where Luther later lived with his wife and family, is a wonderfully vivid museum of the German Reformation. The house of his friend and brother-in-arms, Philip Melanchthon, is also open to the public. The Castle Church, to which Luther nailed his 95 theses attacking the Church in 1517, is less interesting than the Stadtkirche, which has survived with many of its original features intact, including a beautiful altar panel by Lucas Cranach the Elder. He was not merely a painter but Wittenberg's wealthiest citizen and mayor; there are plans to open his studio, the Cranachhöfe, to the public.

LÜBBENAU

Lübbenau is an ideal launching pad for exploring the Spreewald, a scenic wonderland of lakes, canals, farmsteads and country inns. The Spreewaldmuseum is near the 19th-century Schloss. The houses around the Marktplatz are worthy examples of the late baroque, as is the Stadtkirche St Nikolai. An attractive timber-framed building is the only reminder of the old town hall (Rathaus). Also interesting is a Saxon milepost that dates from the 18th century.

Lübbenau, on the River Spree, is an embarkation point for boat trips and has a small harbour.

BRANDENBURG

Dominsel is the charmingly understated focal point of the historic centre of the state of Mark Brandenburg. It was here that the first Slav settlers arrived in the 6th century, later founding the Romanesque cathedral (Dom), built on an island in the River Havel. This beautiful building survives in its 14th-century Gothic transformation and should not be missed. If this part of the town has a tranquil, almost forgotten air, the Old Town (Altstadt) is more closely attuned to the modern world, although there are attractions here too, notably the market place (Markt) with its late Gothic town hall (Rathaus). The New Town (Neustadt) was founded in the late 12th century. There are plenty of shops and cafés in its pedestrian zone, but the highlight is the Katherinenkirche in the market place, with medieval sculptures and ceiling paintings. The countryside around Brandenburg is outstanding. Lake Beetzsee, where regattas often take place, is popular and accessible.

INFORMATION

Brandenburg

🚆 From Friedrichstrasse or Zoologischer Garten (trains every hour)

➕ Off map to west

Distance 60km west of Berlin

Journey time About 45 minutes

🏠 Hauptstrasse 51

☎ (03381) 223743

❓ Town centre best explored on foot.
Boat trips on the River Havel.
Public transport

The Brandenburger Roland guards the late-Gothic town hall

What's On

On any given day, Berlin may have 250 exhibitions, while there are over 400 independent theatre groups, 170 museums, 200 art galleries and more than 150 auditoriums. It's not surprising that Berlin's listing magazines (► 92) are among the fattest in Europe.

January	*New Year*: Traditional celebrations at the Brandenburg Gate and gala evening at Staatsoper. *6-Day Race*: Event for cyclists. Velodrom, Landsberger Allee.
February	*International Film Festival (Berlinale)*: The world's film-makers come to Potsdamer Platz.
May	*German Women's Open*: Tennis tournament. LTTC Rot Weiss in Grunewald.
June	*Fête de la Musique*: Open-air concerts featuring music from rock to classical at Brandenburg Gate, Hakesche Höfe and other venues. *Christopher Street Day*: Gay and lesbian procession.
July	*Love Parade*: 'The largest rave party in the world.' More than 1.5 million young people participate. Strasse des 17 Juni, Tiergarten.
September	*Berliner Festwochen*: A month of opera, music, theatre and painting throughout the city.
September/October	*Berlin Marathon*.
October	*German Unity Day* (October 3): Street festival on Unter den Linden.
November	*Anniversary of the opening of the Berlin Wall* (9 November). *JazzFest Berlin*: Good jazz concerts citywide.
December	*Christmas markets*: All month at Opernpalais (Unter den Linden 5), Breitscheidplatz, Alexanderplatz, Winterfeldplatz (Sundays only) and Spandau Altstadt.

BERLIN's
top 25 sights

The sights are shown on the maps on the inside front cover and inside back cover, numbered **1**–**25** from west to east across the city

1 Sanssouci *24*

2 Cecilienhof *25*

3 Klein-Glienicke *26*

4 Spandau Zitadelle *27*

5 Jagdschloss Grunewald *28*

6 Sachsenhausen *29*

7 Ethnologisches Museum *30*

8 Schloss Charlottenburg *31*

9 Kurfürstendamm *32*

10 Kaiser-Wilhelm-Gedächtniskirche *33*

11 Bauhaus-Archiv *34*

12 Kulturforum *35*

13 Kunstgewerbemuseum *36*

14 Tiergarten *37*

15 Topographie des Terrors *38*

16 Brandenburger Tor *39*

17 Checkpoint Charlie *40*

18 Gendarmenmarkt *41*

19 Unter den Linden *42*

20 Museumsinsel *43*

21 Pergamon Museum *44*

22 Berliner Dom *45*

23 Nikolaiviertel *46*

24 Alexanderplatz *47*

25 Schloss Köpenick *48*

Sanssouci

HIGHLIGHTS

- Schloss Sanssouci
- Terraces and Great Fountain
- Grave of Frederick the Great
- Neptune grotto
- Orangery
- Friedenskirche
- Sicilian gardens
- Roman Baths (Römische Bäder)
- New Palace
- Ape bearing Voltaire's features, on the Chinese Teahouse

INFORMATION

- Off map to southwest; Locator map off C4
- Maulbeerallee, Potsdam
- (0331) 9694190
- Schloss Sanssouci: Apr–Oct daily 9–12:30, 1–5. Nov–Mar daily 9–12:30, 1–4. Closed Mon New Palace: Apr–Oct daily 9–12:30, 1–5. Nov–Mar daily 9–12:30, 1–4. Closed Mon
- Café; restaurant
- S-Bahn Potsdam Stadt
- Bus 695, 612, 692
- Wild Park
- Few
- Park free Schloss expensive (guided tour only) New Palace moderate
- Cecilienhof (▶ 25)

Frederick the Great's celebrated Sanssouci was a place of relaxation and peaceful seclusion where the Prussian monarch could get away from it all. The eccentric Chinese Teahouse epitomises his ideal.

Two palaces On the western edge of Potsdam, just 12 miles from Berlin (about 30 minutes by train or car), you'll find landscaped Sanssouci Park. It contains two quite different yet equally impressive palaces built for Frederick the Great. Formal gardens, terraces, fountains, and follies complete the picture. Don't be put off by the crowds around Schloss Sanssouci. Other sights and the grounds are much less congested.

Schloss Sanssouci Frederick's celebrated retreat was designed by a friend, Georg Wenzeslaus von Knobelsdorff. The single-storey rococo façade, topped by a shallow green dome, conceals a succession of gorgeously furnished rooms and a collection of precious objects including sculptures, painted vases and elaborate clocks. The French philosopher Voltaire was Sanssouci's most famous guest – eventually he fell out with Frederick, who said disparagingly 'he has the slyness and will of an ape.'

New Palace If Sanssouci is the perfect reflection of Frederick the Great's cultivated side, then the New Palace (Neues Palais) reveals his obsession with self-aggrandisement. The best view of the expansive red-brick façade is from the imposing driveway, intended both to intimidate and impress courtiers and foreign visitors. Johann Büring designed the façade, and Karl von Gontard the sumptuous interior. About a dozen of the palace's more than 200 rooms are open to the public.

Cecilienhof

A trip to Potsdam Town, rewarding in itself, can easily be combined with an excursion to this unusual palace, which, in July 1945, hosted the Potsdam Conference while Berlin and its environs lay in ruins.

Potsdam Conference Set just north of Potsdam in an area of parkland called the Neuer Garten, Schloss Cecilienhof was the setting for the last great inter-Allied government conference of World War II, ostensibly convened to redraw the post-war map of Europe. The leading delegates were the so-called 'Big Three': Winston Churchill, representing Great Britain; Harry S. Truman of the United States; and, heading the Soviet delegation, Josef Stalin. You can see the conference hall and the studies and reception rooms of the various delegations.

Semi-rural retreat Schloss Cecilienhof, completed in 1917, was commissioned by Kaiser Wilhelm II for his son Wilhelm. Ironically this semi-rural retreat, constructed during World War I, was built in the style of an English country house. The Hohenzollerns occupied the palace until 1945.

Grounds Much older than the palace itself are the buildings on the grounds, notably the Marmorpalais, conceived by Karl von Gontard in 1787–89. Grapevines grew here in abundance – there were more than 40 vineyards in the 18th century. The Dutch-style servants' quarters mirror the style of the celebrated Dutch Quarter in Potsdam Town. Also of interest are the original garden houses, orangery and ruined library.

HIGHLIGHTS

- Conference table
- Offices of the three powers
- Tudor-style chimneys
- Marmorpalais
- Ruined library
- Shingle House
- Carved oak staircase
- Sphinx on the Orangery

INFORMATION

- ✚ Off map to southwest; Locator map off C4
- ⊠ Neuer Garten
- ☎ (0331) 9694244
- 🕐 Nov–Mar daily 9–12:30, 1–4.Apr–Oct daily 9–12:30, 1–5.Closed Mon
- 🍴 Restaurant
- Ⓢ S-Bahn Potsdam-Stadt
- 🚌 Bus 694
- 🚉 Potsdam-Stadt
- ♿ None
- 💰 Moderate

Cecilienhof's 'Tudor' chimneys

Klein-Glienicke

HIGHLIGHTS

- Ornamental gardens
- Lion fountain
- Casino with pergolas
- Relics from the Temple of Poseidon
- Rotunda (Grosse Neugierde)
- Teahouse (Kleine Neugierde)
- Stibadium, pavilion
- Klosterhof
- Glienicker Bridge
- View of Havel

INFORMATION

- ✛ Off map to southwest; Locator map C4
- ✉ Königstrasse 36
- ☎ 8053041
- 🕓 Park: 7AM–8PM daily Schloss: Closed until mid-May 2001
- 🍽 Excellent restaurant
- 🚇 S-Bahn Wannsee
- 🚌 Bus 116, A16
- 🚉 Potsdam-Stadt
- ♿ None
- 💶 Free
- ⟳ Cecilienhof (➤ 25)

The park surrounding this elegant villa and former royal residence is perched decoratively on the banks of the Jungfernsee, between Berlin and Potsdam. Just outside the park gate is the Glienicker Bridge, famous as a setting for Cold War spy novels.

The Schloss and park The mock-Renaissance Schloss was designed in 1824 by Karl Friedrich Schinkel for Prince Friedrich Karl of Prussia, the brother of Kaiser Wilhelm I. Nowadays the grounds are known for their arcadian follies and ornamental garden. The follies are by Schinkel, and the park was laid out by Peter Lenné, also responsible for the Berlin Tiergarten. Looking for rhyme or reason in the choice of follies is a fruitless exercise, although the themes of Renaissance Italy and Classical Greece can be detected here and there. The most extraordinary flight of fancy must be the Klosterhof. These remains are genuinely Italian: the cloister came from a monastery near Venice, while the capital decorated with the chained monkey once belonged to Pisa's famous Leaning Tower.

Glienicker Brücke Just outside the gate is the Glienicker Bridge, which spans the Havel at the southern end of the Jungfernsee to link Berlin with Potsdam. Unremarkable in itself, the bridge came to the world's attention in 1962 when, marking the border between East and West, it was the scene of a swap involving the US pilot Gary Powers, who had been shot down by the Soviet air force on allegations of spying in the famous U-2 incident. The bridge subsequently starred in films and spy novels and became a symbol of the Cold War.

Spandau Zitadelle

Of the many attractive villages on Berlin's outskirts, a favourite is ancient Spandau with its red-brick Zitadelle, picturesque streets, and views across the Havel. The best vantage point is the Juliusturm, the oldest surviving part of the Zitadelle.

The Zitadelle A strategic location at the confluence of the rivers Spree and Havel made Spandau important in the Middle Ages. The first Zitadelle (fortress), dating from the 12th century, was rebuilt by Joachim III in 1557. The oldest surviving part of the building is the crenellated Juliusturm – the view from the top of the tower is worth the steep climb. Most of the bastions and out-buildings date from the 19th-century, though not the Old Magazine, which is as ancient as the castle itself.

Many lives Spandau castle briefly housed a laboratory for developing incendiary rockets in the early 19th century. Now part of it is a museum. One exhibit is an 1860 cannon, brought back from Siberia, where it had languished for more than a century. The fortress last saw active service during the Napoleonic Wars, when the Old Arsenal was reduced to ruins. Just inside the castle gateway is the statue of a defiant Albrecht, the famous Bear of Brandenburg.

Altstadt Spandau The attractive Old Town is only a short walk from the castle. The Gothic house (Gotisches Haus) in Breite Strasse dates from 1232, and in the central square, Reformationsplatz, are cafés and the Nikolaikirche. North of here lies the quaint old area known as the Kolk, and close by is Spandau's busy lock on the Havel.

HIGHLIGHTS

- Cannons
- Statue of Albrecht the Bear
- Museum of the Middle Ages
- Juliusturm
- Bastion walls
- Old Magazine
- Ruined arsenal
- Kolk and Spandau lock

INFORMATION

- ✠ Off map to west; Locator map A4
- ✉ Am Juliusturm
- ☎ 354944200
- 🕐 Tue–Fri 9–5; Sat–Sun 10–5
- 🍴 Am Juliusturm (Zitadelle)(► 62)
- Ⓤ U-Bahn Zitadelle
- 🚌 Bus 133
- 🚉 Spandau
- ♿ Few ▦ Moderate

Detail on the Zitadelle

Jagdschloss Grunewald

HIGHLIGHTS

Jagdschloss Grunewald
- Hunting museum
- *Adam and Eve and Judith*, Lucas Cranach the Elder
- *Susannah and the Elders*, Jacob Jordaens
- *Julius Caesar*, Rubens
- Wooden ceiling in Great Hall
- Trompe-l'oeil stonework

Grunewald Forest
- Grunewaldsee
- Grunewaldturm

INFORMATION

Jagdschloss Grunewald

- ✚ Off map to west; Locator map B3
- ✉ Am Grunewaldsee, near Hüttenweg
- ☎ 8133597
- 🕐 Mid-May–mid-Oct Tue–Sun 10–5. Mid-Oct–mid-May Sat–Sun only 10–4
- 🍴 None
- 🚌 Bus 115, 183
- ♿ None
- 💲 Inexpensive
- ↔ Brücke Museum (➤ 52)

Grunewaldturm

- ✚ Off map to west; Locator map B3
- ✉ Havelchaussee 61
- ☎ 3041203
- 🕐 Tower: daily 10AM–11PM
- 🍴 Café 🕐 Daily 11–11
- 🚌 Bus A18 ♿ None
- 💲 Inexpensive

The Grunewald forest is an amazing woodland on the western edge of Berlin. The dreamily scenic 32sq km, dotted with lakes, beaches and nature reserves, are a favourite playground of Berliners at weekends.

Hunting lodge Jagdschloss Grunewald is an attractive Renaissance hunting lodge, built in 1542 for Elector Joachim II of Brandenburg. The stables and outbuildings date from around 1700, when the house was surrounded by a moat. Today the lodge is a museum decorated with paintings and furniture from various royal collections; the chase is the predominant theme. One picture shows Kaiser Wilhelm on a visit to the Grunewald. The 17th-century Dutch school is well represented among the paintings on display, but the best work is by a German, Lucas Cranach the Elder, who has an entire room to himself. Equally remarkable is the painted wooden ceiling of the Great Hall (Grosser Saal) on the ground floor. This is the only surviving 16th-century room. Across the courtyard, the barn has been converted into a hunting museum.

Grunewald Forest Native trees, felled for fuel after the war, have been replanted. Paths criss-cross the forest, beaches fringe the Havel and there is space for leisure pursuits from boating to hang-gliding. You can swim in the Grunewaldsee, site of the hunting lodge, and in the Krumme Lanke. Between these two lakes is a marshy nature reserve known as the Langes Luch. For views, climb the Grunewaldturm, a 72m folly on the banks of the Havel, built for Kaiser Wilhelm II in 1897. A second vantage point is the Teufelsberg (Devil's Mountain), an artificial hill made from wartime rubble.

Sachsenhausen

Some 100,000 prisoners perished at this concentration camp during World War II. The great lie 'Work makes you free', inscribed on the entrance gate is a chilling reminder of the deception and evil once practised here.

Nerve centre The Nazis opened the camp in July 1936, just as Berlin was preparing to host the Olympic Games. Sachsenhausen was the headquarters of the concentration camp inspectorate, and there was a training school here.

Museums The two museums tell the terrible story of the camp. One focuses on the plight of the Jews; the other, in the former kitchens, displays various artefacts and other illustrations of daily life. Some of the cells in the cell block have been restored in memory of the heroes of the German and international resistance to Fascism. Outside are three wooden execution posts.

Sachsenhausen today

Extermination camp Two of the original prison huts have been preserved, as well as the perimeter walls, parade ground, fences and watchtowers. 'Station Z', where prisoners were murdered – some were shot, some were gassed – before their bodies were cremated, occupies one corner of the site. The furnishings and tiled walls of the pathology department have been preserved. Here corpses were dissected for experimental purposes. Films on various aspects of camp history are shown in the former laundry.

INFORMATION

- Off map to northwest; Locator map off A3
- Strasse der Nationen 22
- (03301) 200200
- Tue–Sun 8.30–4:30
- None
- S-Bahn Oranienburg (then 20-minute walk)
- Bus 804 (then 20-minute walk)
- Oranienburg
- Few
- Free

Ethnologisches Museum

HIGHLIGHTS

- Polynesian clubhouse
- Oceanian boats
- Pre-Columbian gold statuettes
- Peruvian pottery
- Throne and footstool from Cameroon
- Benin bronzes
- Indonesian shadow puppets
- Sri Lankan carved masks
- Australian bark painting
- World music headphones

INFORMATION

- ✚ Off map to south; Locator map B3
- ✉ Lansstrasse 8
- ☎ 20905555 (info)
- 🕐 Tue–Fri 10–6, Sat–Sun 11–6
- 🍴 Café
- 🚇 U-Bahn Dahlem-Dorf
- 🚌 Bus 110, 183, X11, X83
- 🚉 Lichterfelde West
- ♿ Good
- 💷 Moderate
- ↔ Botanischer Garten (➤ 56)

The folk art theme extends beyond the Ethnological Museum to the nearby Dahlem-Dorf U-Bahn station, where modern primitivist sculptures offer provocative seating. Test them for comfort, then make your own artistic judgment.

Exhibitions Although the airy rooms of the Ethnologisches Museum appear large, there is exhibition space for only a fraction of its 400,000-plus ethnological items. Only Oceania and the Americas are represented by permanent exhibitions. Africa, East Asia and South Asia are covered in temporary displays.

Oceania The Oceanian boats are probably the highlight of the collection. The display includes an 18th-century vessel known as a Tongiaki from Tonga, which resembles a catamaran. For landlubbers there is the fantastically decorated male clubhouse, from the Palau Islands of the western Pacific.

Pre-Columbian art The focus of the American collection is the exhibition of ancient sculptures and figurines, mainly from Mexico and Peru.

Gold was the medium favoured by many of these artists and the craftsmanship represented here is perhaps among the best of its kind in the world. Just as beautiful, and more arresting, are the decorated stone *steles* from Cozumalhuapa (Guatemala) created to fend off evil spirits.

Schloss Charlottenburg

This attractive former royal palace, built in the rococo style, lies in its own grounds only a stone's throw from the heart of Berlin. The highlights of the Schloss itself have to be the gorgeous White Hall and Golden Gallery, in the New Wing.

Royal retreat The Schloss was built over more than 100 years, and its development mirrors the aggrandisement of the Prussian dynasty of Hohenzollern, recalled in the forecourt by Andreas Schlüter's superb equestrian statue of the Great Elector, which once stood outside the Berlin Schloss. The Electress Sophie Charlotte's rural retreat, designed by Arnold Nering in 1695, was transformed into the palace you see today during the reigns of Frederick I and Frederick II by the architect Georg Wenzeslaus von Knobelsdorff. The Great Orangery and Theatre and the Galerie der Romantik (which houses an exhibition of German Romantic painting) form wings of the Palace, as does the Langhans Building, now the Museum of Pre- and Early History.

Riverside grounds Do not leave Schloss Charlottenburg without seeing the delightful grounds, which slope toward the River Spree. The formal French garden is a marked contrast to the landscaped English garden, which houses the Mausoleum built for Queen Luise, and the Belvedere, now a museum devoted to Berlin porcelain. Closer to the palace, do not miss the delightfully idiosyncratic Pavilion, designed by Berlin's best-known 19th-century architect, Karl Friedrich Schinkel.

HIGHLIGHTS

- White Hall
- Golden Gallery
- Gobelin's rooms
- Study and bedchamber of Frederick I
- Galerie der Romantik
- *Embarkation for Cythera,* J-A Watteau (above)
- Statue of the Great Elector
- Schinkel Pavilion
- Great Orangery
- Gardens

A familiar landmark

INFORMATION

- ✚ B5; Locator map D4
- ✉ Charlottenburg, Luisenplatz
- ☎ Schloss: 320911. Galerie der Romantik: 20905555 (info)
- 🕐 Tue–Sun 10–5
- 🍴 Restaurant
- 🚇 U-Bahn Richard-Wagner-Platz
- 🚌 Bus 109, 210, X21
- ♿ Few
- 💶 Moderate

31

Kurfürstendamm

HIGHLIGHTS

- Literaturhaus
- Käthe-Kollwitz-Museum
- Wertheim department store (➤ 70)
- Café Kranzler (➤ 68)
- Fasanenstrasse
- Iduna House
- Bristol Hotel Kempinski (➤ 84)
- Neoclassical news-stands

INFORMATION

- ➕ E7; Locator map F4
- 🚇 U-Bahn Uhlandstrasse
- 🚌 Bus 109, 119, 129, 219
- 🚉 Zoologischer Garten
- ↔ Kaiser-Wilhelm-Gedächtniskirche (➤ 33)

Literaturhaus and Wintergarten Café
- ✉ Fasanenstrasse 23
- ☎ 8825414
- 🕐 Daily 9:30AM–1AM
- 🍴 Excellent
- ♿ Few
- 🎟 Free

Käthe-Kollwitz-Museum
- ✉ Fasanenstrasse 24
- ☎ 8825210
- 🕐 Wed–Mon 11–6
- ♿ Few
- 🎟 Moderate

It would be unthinkable to come to Berlin without visiting the Ku'damm, which stretches for three kilometres towards Charlottenburg. The city's celebrated tree-lined boulevard is usually buzzing with pavement cafés, restaurants and Berlin's major shops.

Shopping street Many of the Ku'damm stores were the beneficiaries of the *Wirtschaftswunder*, the economic miracle of the 1960s, which was brought about partly by American investment.

New West End The elegant streets off the Ku'damm – Fasanenstrasse, for example – were a part of the New West End, which was developed as a residential area at the end of the 19th century. Many of the houses here are now art galleries; an exception is the museum devoted to the life and work of the 20th-century artist Käthe Kollwitz at Fasanenstrasse 24. Next door to the museum is the Literaturhaus, a cultural centre with a secluded garden café, the Wintergarten. The Villa Grisebach at No. 25 is an outstanding example of Jugendstil architecture. A little further away, on the corner of Leibnizstrasse, is another period piece, the Iduna House, whose unmistakable cupola dates from 1907.

Coffee shops Despite rising rents on the Ku'damm, the café tradition in Berlin still lives on in the old name of Kranzler. Johann Georg Kranzler opened the first coffee shop in Berlin in 1835, on the corner of Friedrichstrasse. These days, tourists and literati have taken the place of the Prussian aristocracy who once frequented the many cafés; join them for a while to rest your legs, enjoy a superb coffee and watch the world go by.

Kaiser-Wilhelm-Gedächtniskirche

The blackened ruin of this church – bombed in 1943, now a reminder of the futility of war – casts its shadow over the Ku'damm. Particularly moving is the cross of nails given by the people of Coventry in England, another war-torn city.

War memorial The Gedächtniskirche was Kaiser Wilhelm II's contribution to the developing New West End. Built in 1895 in Romanesque style, it was always rather incongruous in this proudly modern section of the city. No expense was spared on the interior, and the dazzling mosaics are deliberately reminiscent of St Mark's in Venice. After Allied bombs destroyed the church in 1943, the shell was allowed to stand. Poignant in its way, the old building now serves as a small museum focusing on the wartime destruction.

The New Chapel Berliners have denigrated the octagonal chapel and hexagonal stained-glass tower, both uncompromisingly modern (the 'make-up box' and the 'lipstick tube' are favoured nicknames). However, many visitors find peace in the blue-hued chapel, whose stained glass is from Chartres, France. The chapel was designed by Egon Eiermann in the early 1960s.

Breitscheidplatz In shameless contrast, brash Breitscheidplatz proclaims the values of a materialistic culture, only partially redeemed by the colourful street musicians and occasional fund-raising stunts. Nowadays it is a refuge for Berlin's down-and-outs and is routinely targeted by the police. The focus is the Globe Fountain (Weltkugelbrunnen).

HIGHLIGHTS

- Cross of nails
- Surviving mosaics
- Models of city centre
- The Stalingrad Madonna
- Bell tower
- Globe Fountain

INFORMATION

- ✚ E6, Locator map E3
- ✉ Breitscheidplatz
- ☎ 2185023
- ◉ Memorial Hall Museum: Mon–Sat 10–4
  New Chapel: daily 9–7
- 🚇 U- or S-Bahn Zoologischer Garten, Kurfürstendamm
- 🚌 Bus 100, 119, 129, 146
- 🚉 Zoologischer Garten
- ♿ Few
- 🎟 Free

Breitscheidplatz

33

Bauhaus-Archiv

HIGHLIGHTS

- Walter Gropius's building
- Marcel Breuer's leather armchair
- Metal-framed furniture
- Ceramics
- Moholy-Nagy's sculpture *Light-space-modulator*
- Designs and models of Bauhaus buildings
- Paintings by Paul Klee
- Paintings by Kandinsky
- Schlemmer's theatre designs
- Marianne Brandt's tea and coffee set

INFORMATION

- ➕ F6; Locator map E3
- ✉ Klingelhöferstrasse 14
- ☎ 2540020
- 🕐 Wed–Mon 10–5
- 🍴 Café
- Ⓤ U-Bahn Nollendorfplatz
- 🚌 Bus 100, 129, 187, 341
- Bellevue
- ♿ Good
- Moderate
- ↔ Kulturforum (➤ 35), Tiergarten (➤ 37)

Brush up on your knowledge of the history of design by visiting one of Berlin's foremost cultural totems – a museum celebrating the Bauhaus, one of the most influential art and design movements of the 20th century.

End of decoration In the traumatic aftermath of World War I all values, artistic ones included, came under scrutiny. In Germany, the dynamic outcome was the Bauhaus school, founded in 1919 by Walter Gropius in Weimar, the capital of the recently founded Republic. Gropius and his disciples stressed function, rather than decoration, favouring modern materials such as concrete and tubular steel for their versatility and appearance.

Interdisciplinary approach Mass production guaranteed the Bauhaus an unprecedented influence on European and transatlantic architecture and design. Most remarkable, perhaps, was the school's insistence on collaboration between different artistic disciplines. Workshops in metalwork, print and advertising, photography, painting and ceramics were coordinated by a cohort of outstanding team leaders, among them Vassily Kandinsky, Paul Klee, Oskar Schlemmer and Laszlo Moholy-Nagy.

Legacy The revolutionary credentials of the Bauhaus drove it into conflict with the Nazis. Already forced to move to Dessau and then to Berlin, the school closed in 1933 but its influence lives on in the design of furniture and appliances found in many homes today.

Exhibition The display, ranging from furniture to sketches, is housed in a small museum designed by Walter Gropius in 1964.

Kulturforum

Conceived in the 1960s by Hans Scharoun, the Kulturforum complex is controversial as architecture. But no one can dispute the beauty of the collections in the Gemäldegalerie and the Neue Nationalgalerie.

Gemäldegalerie The picture gallery, an outstanding collection, comprises more than 1,450 paintings of the 13th to 18th centuries. Dürer, Hans Holbein, Lucas Cranach the Elder and other German masters are well represented, as are the great Dutch artists Van Eyck, Rogier van der Weyden and Pieter Bruegel. Dutch baroque painting is also prominent, with several outstanding works by Rembrandt, among others. The Italian collection reads like a roll-call of great Renaissance artists: Fra Angelico, Piero della Francesco, Giovanni Bellini and Raphael. Outside, in the sculpture park, you can see works by Henry Moore and others.

Neue Nationalgalerie Designed by Bauhaus architect Mies van der Rohe for the hanging of large canvasses, the New National Gallery concentrates on international modern art. Many leading post-war artists are represented here: Robert Rauschenberg, Roy Lichtenstein, Frank Stella, Joseph Beuys. The lower floor displays work by 20th-century Europeans, including Kirchner, Magritte, Klee, Max Ernst, Otto Dix, de Chirico, Dalí and Picasso.

Musikinstrumenten-Museum In the Museum of Musical Instruments, you'll see almost everything from bagpipes to synthesisers. The world's first bass tuba is here, and don't miss the Orchestron organ. The policy is no-touch, but you can listen to tapes of the instruments in performance on strategically placed headphones.

HIGHLIGHTS

Gemäldegalerie
- *Netherlandish Proverbs,* Bruegel
- *Portrait of Enthroned Madonna and Child,* Botticelli
- *Portrait of Georg Gisze,* Rembrandt

Neue Nationalgalerie
- *Pillars of Society,* Grosz
- *Departure of the Ships,* Klee
- *L'Idée Fixe,* Magritte

INFORMATION

- G6; Locator map E2
- Matthäikircheplatz 8
- Gemäldegalerie: 20905555 (info) Neue Nationalgalerie: 2662662 Musikinstrumenten-Museum: 254810
- Gemäldegalerie: Tue–Thu 10–10, Sun 10–6 Neue Nationalgalerie: Tue–Fri 10–6, Thu 10–10, Sat–Sun 11–6 Musikinstrumenten-Museum: Tue–Fri 9–5, Sat–Sun 10–5
- Cafés
- U- or S-Bahn Potsdamer Platz
- Bus 129, 148, 200, 248
- Good
- Moderate; additional charge for temporary exhibitions in the Neue Nationalgalerie

Kunstgewerbemuseum

HIGHLIGHTS

- 8th-century Burse reliquary
- Frederick Barbarossa's baptismal bowl
- J J Kaendler's Harlequin Group
- Lidded goblet of gold ruby glass from Potsdam
- Lüneburg silver
- Gold elephant fountain from Köln
- Guelph reliquary from Köln
- Majolica love dish from Urbino
- Art-deco stained-glass windows
- 'Wiggle-chair' by Frank Gehry

INFORMATION

- G6; Locator map E2
- Matthäikirchplatz
- 2662902
- Tue–Fri 10–6; Sat–Sun 11–6
- Café
- U- or S-Bahn Potsdamer Platz
- Bus 129, 148, 187, 248, 341
- Good
- Inexpensive
- Bauhaus-Archiv (➤ 34), Kulturforum (➤ 35), Tiergarten (➤ 37)

Berlin's wonderful collection of arts and crafts is in the Museum of Applied Art in the Kulturforum. Look for the 8th-century Burse reliquary of Enger, an enamelled wooden box inlaid with gold and studded with silver, pearls, and precious gems.

Cultural riches The vast collections are arranged chronologically on several floors. Every conceivable kind of applied art is displayed, including gold and silver work, glassware, majolica, jewellery, porcelain, furniture and clothing. A counterpoint to the medieval treasures assembled from churches and abbeys all over Germany is the Lüneburg Town Hall silver, evidence of the great wealth acquired by the burghers of the Hanseatic town in the 15th and 16th centuries.

Kunstkammer The museum's collection is based on the 7,000 objects acquired by the Brandenburg Kunstkammer (Cabinet of Curiosities) from the 17th century onwards. An intriguing item is the Pommersche Kunstschrank, a wonderfully eclectic assortment of objects from surgical instruments to hairbrushes and miniature books. It was assembled between 1610 and 1616 for the Duke of Pommern-Stettin.

Porcelain and art deco Painted figurines from Meissen are the highlight of the porcelain collection. The Jugendstil glass, ceramics and jewellery are gorgeous – look for the intricate ornamental fastener made by Lalique in around 1900. On the ground floor is a display of art-deco furniture.

Porcelain figure dated 1780

Tiergarten

Boating, strolling, jogging, summer concerts, ornamental gardens – this enormous park (202ha) in the centre of Berlin offers all this and more. Look for the antique gas lamps from various European cities along the route from the station to the Landwehrkanal.

Hunting ground *Tiergarten* means 'animal garden', recalling a time when the park was stocked with wild boar and deer for the pleasure of the Prussian aristocracy. It was landscaped by Peter Joseph Lenné in the 1830s and still bears his imprint – remarkably, since the park was almost totally destroyed in World War II.

Siegessäule The Siegessäule (victory column) occupies a prime site on Strasse des 17 Juni, although it originally stood in front of the Reichstag. Erected in 1873 to commemorate Prussian victories against Denmark, Austria and France, the 67m column is decorated with captured cannon. 'Gold Else', the victory goddess on the summit, beloved by Berliners, is waving her laurel wreath wryly towards Paris.

War heroes and revolutionaries The three heroes of the Wars of Unification – Count Otto von Bismarck and Generals Helmut von Moltke and Albrecht von Roon – are fêted with statues to the north of the Siegessäule. Memorials to two prominent revolutionaries, Karl Liebknecht and Rosa Luxemburg, stand beside the Landwehrkanal near Lichtensteinallee. Their bodies were dumped in the canal in 1919 by members of the right-wing Free Corps who had shot them shortly after an abortive Communist uprising.

HIGHLIGHTS

- Zoologischer Garten (➤ 59)
- Kongresshalle
- Carillon
- Bismarck monument
- Schloss Bellevue
- Neuer See
- English Garden
- Soviet War Memorial

INFORMATION

Siegessäule
- ✚ F5; Locator map E2
- ✉ Am Grossen Stern, Strasse des 17 Juni
- ☎ 3912961
- 🕐 Mon–Thu 9:30–6:30, Fri–Sun 9:30–7
- 🍴 Café
- Ⓢ S-Bahn Tiergarten
- 🚌 Bus 100, 187, 341
- ♿ None
- 💲 Inexpensive
- ↔ Bauhaus-Archiv (➤ 34), Kulturforum (➤ 35)
- ❓ Viewing platform (no lift)

The Siegessäule

Topographie des Terrors

The Topography of Terror is an interpretive exhibition on the site of the headquarters of Hitler's secret police. It is sobering to contemplate the size and complexity of the Gestapo, and to stand where so many atrocities were committed.

INFORMATION

Exhibition Housed over the former SS kitchens and canteen, this exhibition of photographs chronicling the rise of the Nazi terror regime, its functioning, and its catastrophic demise, gives solemn insights into the workings of the Führer's administration. Next door was a hotel (used as offices) and, adjoining it, the stately Prinz-Albrecht-Palais, which faced onto Wilhelmstrasse. It was this building, known as Prinz-Albrecht-Strasse 8, that became 'the most feared address in Berlin.' Here, prisoners of the Third Reich, including members of the Resistance, were interrogated and tortured, and from here the apparatus of oppression was administered with eerie, bureaucratic efficiency. Outside the exhibition hall, beneath a canopy, are the foundations of the cells where prisoners were held, tortured and sometimes driven to suicide.

Topography A short distance away, a viewing platform resting on a mound of rubble gives a panoramic view of the entire Government Quarter (Regierungsviertel) between Unter den Linden and the Anhalter Bahnhof, where the various ministries of the Third Reich were located. With the help of photographs, you can place the Prinz-Albrecht-Palais, the former Air Ministry (still standing), the headquarters of Hitler's stormtroopers and the offices of the propaganda newspaper *Der Angriff*.

Brandenburger Tor

The Brandenburg Gate began life as a humble toll-gate, marking the city's western boundary. Today it symbolises the reconciliation of East and West and is the perfect backdrop for commemorative events, celebrations and pop concerts.

Gate of Peace? The gate is the work of Karl Gotthard Langhans and dates from 1788–91. Its neoclassical style echoes the ancient entrance to the Acropolis in Athens, on which it is modelled. Conceived as an Arch of Peace, the Brandenburg Gate has more frequently been used to glorify martial values, as in 1933, when the Nazis' torchlight procession through the arch was intended to mark the beginning of the 1,000-year Reich.

Viktoria *The Quadriga*, a sculpture depicting the goddess Viktoria driving her chariot, was added to the gate by Johann Gottfried Schadow in 1794. In 1806, following the Prussian defeat at Jena, it was moved to Paris by Napoleon. When it was brought back in triumph less than a decade later, Karl Friedrich Schinkel added a wreath of oak leaves and the original iron cross to Viktoria's standard. During the heyday of cabaret in the 1920s, *The Quadriga* was often parodied by scantily clad chorus girls.

Pariser Platz During Berlin's booming 1990s, the adjoining square was transformed. Noteworthy buildings include the Adlon Hotel, the Academy of Arts and the DG Bank.

HIGHLIGHTS

- *The Quadriga*
- Classical reliefs
- Adjoining classical pavilions
- View down Unter den Linden
- View down Strasse des 17 Juni
- 'Room of Silence' (in pavilion)
- Pariser Platz
- Tourist office and shop

The Quadriga

INFORMATION

- ✚ H5; Locator map E2
- ✉ Pariser Platz
- 🕐 Daily 11–6
- 🚆 S-Bahn Unter den Linden, U-Bahn Französische Strasse
- 🚌 Bus 100, 200, 257, 348
- 🚉 Friedrichstrasse
- ♿ None
- 🎫 Free

Checkpoint Charlie

HIGHLIGHTS

- Memorial to Wall victim
- Four-language sign
- Portraits of US and Soviet soldiers
- Sentry box

Haus am Checkpoint Charlie
- Wall graffiti exhibition
- Isetta car
- Hot-air balloon
- Fragment of Wall
- Story of life in a divided city

INFORMATION

- ✚ J6; Locator map E2
- ✉ Friedrichstrasse 43–45
- ☎ 2537250
- 🕐 Daily 9AM–10PM
- 🍴 Café
- Ⓢ U-Bahn Kochstrasse
- 🚌 Bus 129
- 🚆 Yorckstrasse
- ♿ Few
- 💷 Expensive
- ↔ Topographie des Terrors (► 38)

Berlin will be famous for its Wall long after Berliners have consigned it to memory. The exhibition in the Haus am Checkpoint Charlie offers a colourful, if highly commercialised, presentation of the Wall experience.

Confrontation It was at this former border crossing that Soviet and US tanks faced off following the construction of the Wall in August 1961. The original prefabricated sentry box has been replaced with a replica, complete with sandbags and two idealised portraits of US and Soviet servicemen by artist Frank Thiel. A multilingual sign warns: 'You are leaving the American sector'.

Redevelopment Teams of international architects have been drafted to redesign the former no-man's land with instructions to merge the eastern and western parts of the city. New landmarks include the Business Centre by Philip Johnson, the Triangle by Josef Kleihues and the tower block commissioned by GSW (Partnership for Housing Development). Across the road is a lone remnant of 19th-century Berlin, a pharmacy-turned-café known as At the White Eagle.

Haus am Checkpoint Charlie Popular with young people generally, the museum is often crowded. On display are adapted vehicles, trick suitcases and a hot-air balloon used for escapes to the West. This emphasis on the sensational sits uncomfortably with the museum's stated purpose, which is to explore the Wall's human rights implications. To this end, there are exhibitions on the Wall's history, on painters and graffiti artists, and on the non-violent struggle for human rights, from Gandhi to Lech Walesa.

Gendarmenmarkt

This beautiful square comes as a pleasant surprise for visitors who associate Berlin with imperial bombast and Prussian marching bands. Climb the Französischer Dom tower for superb views of the Friedrichstadt.

Konzerthaus Known originally as the Schauspielhaus (theatre), the Konzerthaus was designed by Karl Friedrich Schinkel in 1821. Its predecessor was destroyed by fire during a rehearsal of Schiller's play *The Robbers*, so it is fitting that the playwright's monument stands outside. When the building was restored in the early 1980s after being severely damaged in World War II, the original stage and auditorium were dispensed with to make way for a concert hall with a capacity of 1,850 – hence the change of name. The façade, however, retains Schinkel's original design. Keep an eye out for the sculpture of Apollo in his chariot.

Two cathedrals The twin French and German cathedrals (Französischer Dom and Deutscher Dom) occupy opposite ends of the square. The architect Karl von Gontard was described as an ass by Frederick the Great; one of the complementary cupolas collapsed in 1781. A small museum in the Deutscher Dom charts the history of German democracy from the 19th century to the present with photographs, film and a variety of artefacts. A museum in the Französischer Dom tells the story of the hardworking Huguenots who settled in Berlin in the 17th century, fleeing persecution in France. The Cathedral (minus its baroque tower, a later addition) was built for them. The cathedral's other attractions include the Turmstube restaurant in the tower, and the famous carillon, which plays three times daily.

HIGHLIGHTS

- Konzerthaus
- Statue of Schiller
- Apollo in his chariot
- Deutscher Dom
- Cathedrals' twin towers

Französischer Dom
- Turmstube
- Balustrade view
- Carillon

Konzerthaus

INFORMATION

- ✚ J5; Locator map E2
- ☎ Französischer Dom: 2291760 Deutscher Dom: 22730431
- 🕐 Französischer Dom: daily 10–6. Huguenot Museum: Tue–Sat noon–5; Sun 1–5. Deutscher Dom: Tue–Sun 10–5
- 🚇 U-Bahn Stadtmitte
- 🚌 Bus 100, 147, 257, 348
- 🚉 Friedrichstrasse
- 💷 Inexpensive

41

Unter den Linden

HIGHLIGHTS

- Deutsche Staatsoper
- Façade of Alte-Königliche Bibliothek
- Statue of Frederick the Great
- Humboldt University
- Neue Wache
- Zeughaus (note especially the masks of dying warriors in the Schlüterhof)
- Cannon (in the Schlüterhof)
- Operncafé (➤ 69)
- Hedwigskirche

INFORMATION

- ✚ J5; Locator map E2
- ✉ Unter den Linden 2
- ☎ Deutsches Historisches Museum (German History Museum): 203040
  Hedwigskirche: 2034810
- 🕐 Deutsches Historisches Museum: Thu–Tue 10–6.
  Hedwigskirche: Mon–Sat 10–5; Sun 12:30–5
- 🍴 Operncafé and restaurant
- Ⓤ U-Bahn Französische Strasse
- 🚌 Bus 100, 147, 257
- 🚃 Friedrichstrasse
- ♿ None
- 🎟 Deutsches Historisches Museum: free
- 🔗 Gendarmenmarkt (➤ 41), Museumsinsel (➤ 43), Pergamon Museum (➤ 44), Berliner Dom (➤ 45)

The street 'Under the Linden Trees' – once the heart of imperial Berlin – boasts some fine neoclassical and baroque buildings. The pièce de résistance is Andreas Schlüter's superb sculptures of dying warriors in the courtyard of the Zeughaus.

Forum Fridericianum Frederick the Great presides over the eastern end of Unter den Linden. His equestrian statue, by Daniel Christian Rauch, stands next to Bebelplatz, once known as the Forum Fridericianum and intended by the Prussian monarch to evoke the grandeur of Imperial Rome. Dominating the square is Georg von Knobelsdorff's opera house, the Deutsche Staatsoper. Facing it is the Old Royal Library (Alte-Königliche Bibliothek), completed in 1780 and nicknamed the Kommode (chest of drawers) by quick-witted Berliners. Here, in 1933, Nazi propaganda chief Josef Goebbels consigned the works of ideological opponents to the flames in a public book-burning. Just south of Bebelplatz is the Roman Catholic cathedral, the Hedwigskirche, whose classical lines echo the Pantheon in Rome.

Zeughaus Frederick's civic project was never completed, but the buildings on the opposite side of Unter den Linden keep up imperial appearances. Karl Marx was a student at the Humboldt University, designed by Johann Boumann as a palace for Frederick the Great's brother in 1748. Next comes the Neue Wache (Guardhouse), which Schinkel designed in 1818 to complement Johann Nering's magnificent 1695 baroque palace, the Zeughaus (Arsenal). Until mid-2002, the Deutsches Historisches Museum (German History Museum) will occupy the Kronprinzenpalais opposite.

Museumsinsel

Berlin's famed collection of antiquities, dispersed during World War II, is one of the city's major treasures. To see it, head for Museums Island, accessible over the Monbijou Bridge, in the Spree. The Pergamon (➤ 44) is one of five superb institutions there.

Altes Museum Built in 1830, this was the first museum on the island. Karl Schinkel's magnificent classical temple shares with the Pergamon (➤ 44) fabulous collections of sculptures, paintings and artefacts from all corners of the ancient world. The building itself accorded with Schinkel's vision of Berlin as Athens on the Spree. The impression made by the façade is overwhelming, and hidden at the core of the building is a rotunda inspired by Rome's Pantheon and lined with statues of the gods.

Neues Museum Beginning in 2005 Berlin's famed Egyptian collections will be housed once again in this museum, designed in 1843 by August Stüler. Treasures include the bust of Queen Nefertiti currently in Charlottenburg (➤ 50); she may be reunited with a similar bust of her husband, King Akhenaten.

Bode-Museum Named after Wilhelm von Bode (1845–1929), for 20 years curator of Museums Island, this 1904 building will exhibit exquisite medieval sculptures (including works by German master Tilman Riemenschneider), early Christian and Byzantine art, and a superb coin collection. Scheduled to reopen in 2004.

Alte Nationalgalerie This gallery, opening late 2001, displays mainly paintings of the 19th century, and includes works by Impressionists such as Manet, Monet, Degas and Cézanne.

HIGHLIGHTS

- View of Altes Museum from the Lustgarten
- Rotunda of Altes Museum
- *Unter den Linden*, Franz Krüger (Alte Nationalgalerie)
- *Portrait of Frederick the Great at Potsdam*, Adolph Menzel (Alte Nationalgalerie)
- View from Monbijou Bridge

INFORMATION

- J5; Locator map D1
- Museumsinsel
- 20905555 (info)
- While rebuilding continues, some museums are open only for temporary exhibitions Tue–Sun 10–6
- Café Pergamon (➤ 44)
- S-Bahn Hackescher Markt
- Bus 100, 157
- Hackescher Markt
- Few
- Moderate
- Pergamon Museum (➤ 44), Berliner Dom (➤ 45)

Schinkel's Rotunda, the Altes Museum

Pergamon Museum

HIGHLIGHTS

- 120m frieze on Pergamon Altar
- Market gate from Miletus
- Ishtar Gate
- Façade of Mshatta Palace
- Nebuchadnezzar's throne room
- Figurines from Jericho
- Panelled room from Aleppo
- Bust of the Emperor Caracalla
- Statue of Aphrodite from Myrina
- Mosaic from Hadrian's villa at Tivoli

INFORMATION

- J5; Locator map D1
- Am Kupfergraben, Museumsinsel
- 20905555 (info)
- Tue–Sun 9–5; large halls also open Mon–Tue
- Café
- S-Bahn Hackescher Markt
- Bus 100, 157, 200, 348
- Hackescher Markt
- Few
- Moderate
- Unter den Linden
  (➤ 42), Museumsinsel
  (➤ 43), Berliner Dom
  (➤ 45)

If you have time to visit only one museum in Berlin, choose the Pergamon. Virtually every corner of the ancient world is represented, from the Roman Empire to the Islamic world.

Controversy Like the other museums on Museums Island (Museumsinsel), the Pergamon was built to house the vast haul of antiquities amassed by German archaeologists in the 19th century. Controversy rages in museum circles over the proper home for such relics; some people argue that they were wrongfully plundered and have no place in Western museums.

Pergamon Altar The museum's most stunning exhibit is the famous Pergamon Altar from Asia Minor, a stupendous monument so huge that it needs a hall more than 15m high to accommodate it. From Bergama on the west coast of Turkey, it was excavated by Carl Humann in 1878–86. Dating from about 164 BC, it was actually part of a complex of royal palaces, temples, a library and a theatre. Hardly less impressive is the reconstructed market gateway of Miletus, built by the Romans in this town in western Turkey in AD 120 during the reign of Emperor Hadrian. The Babylonian Ishtar Gate makes a startling contrast with its brilliantly coloured bricks of glazed clay. Built between 604 and 562 BC, it was dedicated to the goddess of war, Ishtar, whose symbol was a lion.

Antiquities The museum also has a splendid collection of Greek and Roman statues (some of them retaining traces of their original vibrant colouring), Islamic art, figurines and clay tablets. Many more artefacts come from Sumeria and other parts of the Middle East.

Berliner Dom

For evidence of imperial pretensions, look to Berlin's Protestant cathedral. The cathedral's vast vault contains the sarcophagi of more than 90 members of the Hohenzollern dynasty.

Cathedral Architect Julius Raschdorff built the Berliner Dom over the site of a smaller imperial chapel. The existing cathedral was completed in 1905 and opened in the presence of Kaiser Wilhelm II. Inside, the most impressive feature is the 74m-high dome, supported by pillars of Silesian sandstone and decorated with mosaics of the Beatitudes by Anton von Werner. In High Renaissance style, its huge dome, open to the public and reached by climbing 270 steps, is reminiscent of St Peter's in Rome. The cathedral was badly damaged during World War II, but restoration started in 1974 after years of neglect and is now well advanced. Work on the stained-glass windows has been completed.

Destroyed by Allied bombs The name of the square, Lustgarten, derives from the former pleasure garden which stood just outside the cathedral on Museumsinsel. The site, where the Great Elector is said to have planted potatoes, is now covered by grass and paving. Opposite, until the Allied bombings in World War II, stood the enormous Berliner Schloss, dating from the early 18th century and designed by Andreas Schlüter and Johann Eosander von Göethe. The statue of the Great Elector, now in front of Schloss Charlottenburg, once stood here. There has been a campaign to have the Berliner Schloss rebuilt. The cost, however, will surely be prohibitive.

HIGHLIGHTS

- Lustgarten
- High Renaissance-style façade
- Baptism chapel
- Imperial staircase
- Sarcophagi
- 74m-high dome
- Carved figures above altar
- Restoration viewing gallery

INFORMATION

- ✚ K5; Locator map D1
- ✉ Am Lustgarten
- ☎ 20269136
- 🕐 Mon–Sat 9–7; Sun noon–7
- 🍴 None
- Ⓤ U-Bahn Hausvogteiplatz
- 🚌 Bus 100, 157
- 🚊 Hackescher Markt
- ♿ Few
- 💲 Moderate
- ❓ Organ recitals daily May–Sep 3PM

The Dom from Marx-Engels-Forum

Nikolaiviertel

HIGHLIGHTS

Nikolaikirche
- Exhibition of Berlin history
- Gothic nave
- *The Good Samaritan*, Michael Ribestein
- Hunger Cloth (in vestry)
- Wooden *Crucifixion* of 1485

Nikolaiviertel
- Knoblauchhaus
- Ephraimpalais
- Zum Nussbaum (➤ 69)
- Well outside the pub Zum Paddenwirt

INFORMATION

- K5; Locator map E1
- ✉ Poststrasse
- ☎ Nikolaikirche: 24002182
  Knoblauchhaus: 24002171
  Ephraimpalais: 24002121
- 🕔 Nikolaikirche: Tue–Sun 10–6
  Knoblauchhaus: Tue–Sun 10–6
  Ephraimpalais: Tue–Sun 10–6
- 🍴 Excellent café; restaurant
- Ⓤ U-Bahn Klosterstrasse
- 🚌 Bus 100, 142, 157 257
- 🚊 Alexanderplatz
- ♿ Few
- 🎟 Nikolaikirche: moderate
  Knoblauchhaus: moderate
  Ephraimpalais: moderate
- ⟷ Berliner Dom (➤ 45), Alexanderplatz (➤ 47)

Step back two or three centuries and enjoy a wander through the Nikolai Quarter, a diverting pastiche of baroque and neoclassical architecture, with rows of gabled houses, cobbled streets and quaint shops.

Nikolaikirche The dominating landmark is the twin-spired church that gives the Nikolaiviertel its name. The Nikolaikirche is the oldest church in Berlin, dating originally from 1200 although the present building was not completed until 1470. Seriously damaged in World War II, the beautifully proportioned Gothic nave has been sensitively restored. The church is of great historic importance, because it was here, in 1307, that the two communities of Berlin and Cölln were formally united. The church, now used for services only occasionally, houses a museum of Berlin history that includes models of the medieval city.

Around the Quarter Two other notable buildings recall the lavish lifestyle of Imperial Berlin. The pink stuccoed Knoblauchhaus was designed in 1759 by Friedrich Wilhelm Dietrichs for one of Berlin's most distinguished families. The family's history is illustrated in a small museum with paintings and Biedermeier furniture. The extravagant Ephraimpalais in rococo style, with golden balconies and stone cherubs, once belonged to Frederick the Great's banker, Nathan Ephraim. The interior is decorated with art of the 17th to the 19th centuries.

Most picturesque Among streets, the title probably goes to Eiergasse and Am Nussbaum, named for its cheery reconstruction of a famous 16th-century Berlin inn, Zum Nussbaum ('At the Nut Tree') – a good refreshment stop.

Alexanderplatz

A victim of East German town planning, 'Alex' (as Berliners affectionately call this historic old market place) is waiting to be revamped by a new generation of architects with a mandate to return it to the people.

Historic square Alexanderplatz is named after Russian Tsar Alexander I, who once reviewed troops here. The square was colonised by Berlin's burgeoning working class in the middle of the 19th century. Crime flourished, so it is no accident that the police headquarters was near by.

TV tower The Fernsehturm rises like an unlovely flower from the centre of the square. Its single virtue is its great height, which at 362m exceeds even that of Paris's Eiffel Tower. Climb it on a fine day for panoramic city views. The cost of Hans Kolhoff's ambitious plans for the eventual development of the square may be prohibitive.

Fernsehturm and City Hall

Other attractions Two historic buildings add lustre to the edges of Alexanderplatz. City Hall was formerly known as the Rotes Rathaus (Red Town Hall) because of its colour. Architect Heinrich Friedrich Waesemann was inspired by the municipal architecture of Renaissance Italy when he designed the building in 1869. The Marienkirche, Berlin's second-oldest church, is a survivor from an earlier age. The nave is 15th-century, and the lantern tower a flight of fancy added by Karl Gotthard Langhans in 1790. An epidemic of the plague in 1484 is commemorated in a large medieval wall painting entitled *Totentanz* (*Dance of Death*).

HIGHLIGHTS

- Fernsehturm
- City Hall
- World Time Clock
- Neptune Fountain
- Forum Hotel
- Kaufhof department store (➤ 70)
- Marienkirche
- *Totentanz* (*Dance of Death*) wall painting

INFORMATION

- K5; Locator map D1
- ☎ Fernsehturm: 2423333
- ◷ Fernsehturm: daily 9AM–12:30AM
  Marienkirche: Mon–Thu 10–noon, 1–4 ; Sat noon–4
- 🍴 Cafés; Fernsehturm restaurant with view
- Ⓤ U- or S-Bahn Alexanderplatz
- 🚌 Bus 100, 157, 200, 348
- ♿ Fernsehturm: moderate

47

Schloss Köpenick

HIGHLIGHTS

- Dutch baroque façade
- Stucco ceiling of the Wappensaal
- Collection of gold and silver tableware
- Swiss panelled room
- Jugendstil glass
- 18th-century furniture
- Baroque chapel
- Schlossinsel
- View of the old fishing port of Kietz

INFORMATION

- ✚ Off map to southeast; Locator map C1
- ✉ Schlossinsel
- ◉ Closed for renovation until 2002
- 🍽 Café **⌖** None
- Ⓢ S-Bahn Köpenick
- 🚌 Bus 167, 360
- 🚊 Köpenick
- 🐌 Inexpensive
- ℹ Alt Köpenick 34
- ☎ 6557550

Standing in peaceful parkland on the Schlossinsel, at the confluence of the Dahme and Spree, this time-worn 17th-century former residence of the rulers of the Mark Brandenburg has its own offbeat charm.

Royal residence The current Schloss, built in the Dutch baroque style by Rutger van Langefelt for Elector Friedrich in 1681, stands on the site of a 9th-century Slav fortress. Its most remarkable feature is the Hall of Arms (Wappensaal), whose stuccoed ceiling is by Italian artisan Giovanni Carove. Classical figures support the coats of arms of the Mark Brandenburg. The chapel, dating from 1682–85, is a distinguished example of Arnold Nering's work.

Museum The Schloss also houses a branch of the Kunstgewerbemuseum (Museum of Applied Art ➤ 36). The display includes silverware rescued from the ruins of the Berlin Royal Palace at the end of World War II. There is furniture by David Roentgens, including an elegant cabinet dating from 1779, a small but fine collection of glassware, and a dinner service belonging to Frederick II, manufactured by the famous Royal Porcelain Factory.

Köpenick Köpenick was a hotbed of working-class resistance to the Nazis. More than 90 people perished during Blutwoche, the 'blood week' in 1933, and many others were imprisoned and tortured. A memorial in Puchanstrasse commemorates the events. Today the old town (Altstadt) is undergoing extensive restoration. Its dilapidated but picturesque streets, dating from the 13th century, retain an antique flavour and are worth exploring.

The Dutch baroque façade

BERLIN's
best

Museums *50–51*

Galleries *52*

Places of Worship *53*

Bridges *54*

Political Sights *55*

Parks & Gardens *56*

Views *57*

Statues & Monuments *58*

For Children *59*

What's Free *60*

49

Museums

CITY OF MUSEUMS

Berlin's museums are justifiably renowned the world over for their comprehensiveness and diversity. Many subjects still have two collections devoted to them – one from the East and one from the West. This situation arose amid the confusion of the divided city after World War II, when many of the artefacts were stolen or dispersed and had to be brought back together again. The fantastic archaeological finds of the 19th century, brought here by the cartload, make the museums specialising in antiquities a treat.

In the Top 25

- **19 DEUTSCHES HISTORISCHES MUSEUM (GERMAN HISTORY MUSEUM ➤ 42)**
- **7 ETHNOLOGISCHES MUSEUM (ETHNOLOGICAL MUSEUM), DAHLEM (➤ 30)**
- **17 HAUS AM CHECKPOINT CHARLIE (CHECKPOINT CHARLIE MUSEUM ➤ 40)**
- **16 HISTORICAL EXHIBITION IN DEUTSCHER DOM (➤ 41)**
- **16 HUGENOTTENMUSEUM (HUGUENOT MUSEUM), IN FRANZÖSISCHER DOM (➤ 41)**
- **13 KUNSTGEWERBEMUSEUM (MUSEUM OF APPLIED ART), KULTURFORUM (➤ 36)**
- **12 MUSIKINSTRUMENTEN-MUSEUM (MUSEUM OF MUSICAL INSTRUMENTS), KULTURFORUM (➤ 35)**
- **21 PERGAMON MUSEUM (➤ 44)**

ÄGYPTISCHES MUSEUM (EGYPTIAN MUSEUM)

The undisputed star of this rich collection is the bust of Tutankhamen's aunt, Queen Nefertiti, dating from about 1340 BC. There are also mummies, death masks, jewellery and even games.

🔳 C5 ✉ Schlossstrasse 70 ☎ 34357336 🕓 Tue–Sun 10–6 🚌 Bus 109, 157, 210 Ⓤ U-Bahn Sophie-Charlotte-Platz 🎟 Moderate

ALLIIERTEN-MUSEUM (ALLIED FORCES MUSEUM)

The former US mission plays host to this exhibition on the Allied occupation of Berlin.

🔳 Off map to the south ✉ Clayallee 135 ☎ 8181990 🕓 Tue–Sun 10–6 Ⓤ U-Bahn Oskar-Helene-Heim 🎟 Free

Bust of Queen Nefertiti, Egyptian Museum

BRECHT-HAUS (BRECHT'S HOUSE)

The famous German playwright Bertolt Brecht (1898–1956) lived in this house for the last three years of his life. Archive material on Brecht is kept here.

🔳 H4 ✉ Chausseestrasse 125 ☎ 283057044 🕓 Tue–Fri 10–noon; Thu 10–noon and 5–7; Sat 9:30–noon and 12:30–2 Ⓤ U-Bahn Zinnowitzerstrasse 🎟 Moderate; guided tour only

BRÖHAN MUSEUM

In 1983, Professor Karl Bröhan presented his superb collection of Jugendstil and art deco crafts to the city. The highlight of the museum is a series of rooms decorated in the styles of the leading designers of the period.

🔳 B5 ✉ Schlossstrasse 1a ☎ 32690600 🕓 Tue–Sun 10–6 🚌 Bus 109, 157, 210 Ⓤ U-Bahn Sophie-Charlotte-Platz 🎟 Moderate

German Technology
Museum

DEUTSCHES TECHNIKMUSEUM (GERMAN TECHNOLOGY MUSEUM)

A thoroughly entertaining and beautifully presented exhibition in the locomotive sheds of the old Anhalter train station. Everything from biplanes and vintage cars to model ships and computers.

✚ H7 ✉ Trebbiner Strasse 9 ☎ 254840 ⊙ Tue–Fri 9–5:30; Sat–Sun 10–6 ⊙ U-Bahn Gleisdreieck 💵 Moderate

FILMMUSEUM BERLIN (FILM MUSEUM)

A fascinating journey through the history of German film from 1895. Includes a special tribute to Marlene Dietrich.

✚ H6 ✉ Potsdamer Strasse 2 ☎ 3009030 ⊙ Tue–Sun 10–6; Thu 10–8 ⊙ U- or S-Bahn Potsdamer Platz 💵 Expensive

JÜDISCHES MUSEUM (JEWISH MUSEUM)

This controversial new building by Polish-born architect, Daniel Libeskind, contains an exhibition on German–Jewish history from the earliest times to the present day.

✚ J7 ✉ Lindenstrasse 9–14 ☎ 25993300 ⊙ Due to open Sep 2001 ⊙ U-Bahn Kochstrasse 💵 Moderate

MUSEUM FÜR INDISCHE KUNST; OSTASIATISCHE KUNST (MUSEUMS OF INDIAN AND EAST ASIAN ART)

Two museums within a complex of galleries in Dahlem, presenting the art and culture of India and the Far East with style and imagination.

✚ Off map to south ✉ Lansstrasse 8 ☎ 8301382 ⊙ Tue–Fri 10–6; Sat–Sun 11–6 ⊙ U-Bahn Dahlem-Dorf 💵 Moderate

NEUE SYNAGOGE (NEW SYNAGOGUE)

Visible from all over the Mitte on account of its golden dome, this historic building dates from 1866 and is now a centre for Jewish studies. Inside is a moving exhibition on the history of the community.

✚ J4 ✉ Oranienburger Strasse 28–30 ☎ 88028316 ⊙ Mon 10–8; Tue–Thu 10–6; Fri 10–5 ⊙ S-Bahn Oranienburger Strasse 💵 Moderate

THE STORY OF BERLIN

This state-of-the-art exhibition uses 3-D sound systems, touch screens, time tunnels and adventure rooms to tell the story of Berlin from the time of its founding in 1237.

✚ E7 ✉ Kufürstendamm 207–8, Ku'damm, Karree ☎ 018105992010 ⊙ Daily 10–8 ⊙ U-Bahn Uhlandstrasse 💵 Expensive (family card available)

TROY'S TREASURES

Rumours abound concerning the return of Berlin's most famous archaeological treasure, the 10,000 objects recovered by Heinrich Schliemann from the site of what he assumed to be the ancient city of Troy in the 1870s. Rather fancifully, as it turned out, Schliemann attributed the vast hoard of gold to the Homeric hero King Priam himself. The collection disappeared during World War II, but has since been on show in Moscow.

Galleries

DIE BRÜCKE

Anyone wishing for an introduction to 20th-century art could hardly do better than visit the Brücke Museum on the edge of the Grunewald forest. The artistic movement known as Die Brücke (the Bridge), which flourished between 1905 and 1913, was in the vanguard of German Expressionism. The landscapes and portraits by Ludwig Kirchner, Karl Schmidt-Rottluff, Emil Nolde, Max Pechstein and others bridge the gap between figurative and abstract art and make Cubism more comprehensible.

In the Top 25

🔳 **BAUHAUS-ARCHIV (BAUHAUS MUSEUM ➤ 34)**
🔳 **EPHRAIMPALAIS (➤ 46)**
🔳 **GALERIE DER ROMANTIK (GALLERY OF ROMANTIC PAINTING ➤ 31)**
🔳 **GEMÄLDEGALERIE (PICTURE GALLERY), KULTURFORUM (➤ 35)**
🔳 **KÄTHE-KOLLWITZ-MUSEUM (➤ 32)**
🔳 **MUSEUMSINSEL (MUSEUMS ISLAND ➤ 43)**
🔳 **NEUE NATIONALGALERIE (NEW NATIONAL GALLERY), KULTURFORUM (➤ 35)**

BERGGRUEN COLLECTION

A stimulating exhibition of paintings and sculptures by Picasso and his contemporaries. There are nearly 70 pieces by Picasso, as well as works by Klee, Braque, Giacometti and Cézanne.
➕ B5 ✉ Schlossstrasse 1 ☎ 20905555 🕐 Tue–Fri 10–6; Sat–Sun 11–6 🚌 Bus 109, 145, 210 💷 Moderate

BRÜCKE MUSEUM

This small, modern gallery exhibits work from the group of 20th-century German artists known as Die Brücke.
➕ Off map to south ✉ Bussardsteig 9 ☎ 8312029 🕐 Wed–Mon 11–5 🚌 Bus 115 💷 Moderate

Martin-Gropius-Bau

EASTSIDE GALLERY

Graffiti art as revealed on 730m of the former Berlin Wall, on the north bank of the River Spree. It is said to be the world's largest open-air art gallery.
➕ M6 ✉ Mühlenstrasse 🚇 U-Bahn Schlesisches Tor 💷 Free

KUPFERSTICH-KABINETT

The 'engravings room' is a collection of drawings and prints by some of the great European artists, including Cranach, Dürer, Pieter Bruegel the Elder, Rembrandt and Kandinsky.
➕ G6 ✉ Matthäikirchplatz 6 ☎ 2662002 🕐 Tue–Fri 9–4 🚇 U- or S-Bahn Potsdamer Platz 💷 Moderate

MARTIN-GROPIUS-BAU

Designed by architect Martin Gropius in the style of the Italian Renaissance, and an interesting building in itself, this is a venue for major art exhibitions.
➕ H6 ✉ Stresemannstrasse 110 ☎ 254860 🕐 Tue–Sun 10–8 🚇 U-Bahn Potsdamer Platz 💷 Moderate

Places of Worship

In the Top 25

☷ BERLINER DOM (BERLIN CATHEDRAL ➤ 45)
⏸ FRANZÖSISCHER DOM
(FRENCH CATHEDRAL ➤ 41)
⏸ HEDWIGSKIRCHE (➤ 42)
⏸ KAISER-WILHELM-GEDÄCHTNISKIRCHE
(KAISER WILHELM MEMORIAL CHURCH ➤ 33)
⏸ MARIENKIRCHE (➤ 47)
☷ NIKOLAIKIRCHE (➤ 46)

FRIEDRICHWERDERSCHE KIRCHE

Berlin's celebrated architect Karl Friedrich Schinkel designed this church in neo-Gothic style in 1824. It is now a museum honouring his work.

✚ J5 ✉ Werderstrasse ☎ 2081323 ⏰ Tue–Sun 10–6 🚇 U-Bahn Hausvogteiplatz 💲 Moderate

GETHSEMANE KIRCHE

This church shot to fame overnight in 1989 when it became the spiritual centre of the resistance movement to the East German Communist regime. Nightly peace vigils drew the world's media.

✚ L2 ✉ Stargarder Strasse ☎ 442850 for services 🚇 U- or S-Bahn Schönhauser Allee

NEUE SYNAGOGE (NEW SYNAGOGUE)

The stunning dome of this 1866 building is one of Berlin's landmarks. Designed by Eduard Knoblauch and August Stüler, it survived the infamous Kristallnacht on 9 November 1938, when the Nazis destroyed Jewish buildings.

✚ J4 ✉ Oranienburger Strasse 28–30 ☎ 88028316 🚇 S-Bahn Oranienburger Strasse

SOPHIENKIRCHE

Berlin's sole surviving Baroque church, completed in 1734, was designed by J F Grael.

✚ K4 ✉ Grosse Hamburger Strasse 29 ☎ 3087920 ⏰ May–Oct Wed 3–6; Sun 10 (service) 🚇 U-Bahn Weinmeisterstrasse

K F SCHINKEL

No man left more of an impression on the architecture of Berlin than Karl Friedrich Schinkel (1781–1840). He favoured the classical style, as in the Konzerthaus (formerly the Schauspielhaus) and the Neue Wache. But in designing the Friedrichwerdersche Kirche he turned for inspiration to medieval Gothic. The beautifully proportioned nave is the setting for a satisfying exhibition on his life's work.

Inside Friedrich-werdersche Kirche

Bridges

┌─ **In the Top 25** ──────────────
3 **GLIENICKER BRÜCKE** (► 26)
20 **MONBIJOUBRÜCKE** (► 43)

ROSA LUXEMBURG

The most dramatic event to occur at one of Berlin's many bridges was the recovery of the body of communist agitator Rosa Luxemburg in January 1919. After her murder by right-wing army officers in the Tiergarten, her corpse was dumped into the Landwehrkanal. It was found weeks later under the Lichtensteinbrücke.

FRIEDRICHS-BRÜCKE

This elegant bridge, built in 1892, provides a fine view of the Berliner Dom.

➕ K5 ✉ Bodestrasse 🚇 S-Bahn Hackescher Markt

GERTRAUDENBRÜCKE

Gertraud was a favourite saint of the fisherfolk who used to ply the waters here in the Middle Ages. Bronze water rats decorate the base of her statue.

➕ K6 ✉ Gertraudenstrasse 🚇 U-Bahn Spittelmarkt

JUNGFERNBRÜCKE

This drawbridge, dating from 1798, was once the haunt of Huguenot working girls selling silk and lace.

➕ K5 ✉ Friedrichsgracht 🚇 U-Bahn Spittelmarkt

LESSINGBRÜCKE

Gotthold Ephraim Lessing (1729–81) is one of Germany's best-known playwrights. Scenes from his dramas decorate the sandstone piers of 'his' bridge.

➕ F4 ✉ Lessingstrasse 🚇 U-Bahn Turmstrasse

MOABITER BRÜCKE

This bridge of 1864 is famous for the four bears that decorate it. The bear is the symbol of Berlin.

➕ F5 ✉ Bellevue Ufer 🚇 S-Bahn Bellevue

MOLTKEBRÜCKE

Named for a hero of the Franco-Prussian war, this belligerent bridge is guarded by Prussian eagles and cherubs wielding swords, spears, trumpets and drums. It was completed in 1891.

➕ G5 ✉ Willi-Brandt-Strasse 🚇 S-Bahn Lehrter Stadtbahnhof

OBERBAUMBRÜCKE

Over 500 different kinds of tiles were used in the renovation of what was once Berlin's longest bridge.

➕ N7 ✉ Mühlenstrasse 🚇 U-Bahn Schlesisches Tor

SCHLEUSENBRÜCKE

This simple iron bridge is decorated with historic scenes of Berlin.

➕ K5 ✉ Werderstrasse 🚇 U-Bahn Hausvogteiplatz

SCHLOSSBRÜCKE

Karl Friedrich Schinkel designed a new bridge to replace the decrepit Hundebrücke in 1819. Named after a royal palace that no longer exists, it is decorated with statues of Greek gods.

➕ K5 ✉ Unter den Linden 🚇 U-Bahn Hausvogteiplatz

Moltkebrücke

Political Sights

In the Top 25

16 BRANDENBURGER TOR
(BRANDENBURG GATE ➤ 39)
17 CHECKPOINT CHARLIE (➤ 40)
6 SACHSENHAUSEN (➤ 29)
15 TOPOGRAPHIE DES TERRORS
(TOPOGRAPHY OF TERROR ➤ 38)

FEDERAL CHANCELLERY

The Reichstag has a new neighbour. Across Platz der Republik a gleaming white block has been built to provide 370 offices for Chancellor Gerhard Schröder, his team of officials and political assistants. The new Federal Chancellery (Bundeskanzleramt) has been criticised for being too monumental. A few hundred metres away stands Schloss Bellevue, the official residence of Federal President Johannes Rau.

GEDENKSTÄTTE HAUS DER WANNSEE KONFERENZ (WANNSEE CONFERENCE CENTRE)

In this innocuous-looking mansion on the shores of Lake Wannsee, leading Nazis plotted the mass extermination of Europe's 11 million Jews. The exhibition tells the whole horrific story.

➕ Off map to southwest ✉ Am Grossen Wannsee 58 ☎ 8050010
🕐 Daily 10–6 🚉 S-Bahn Wannsee 🚌 Bus 114 💵 Free

RATHAUS SCHÖNEBERG (SCHÖNEBERG TOWN HALL)

From 1948 to 1989 this was the municipal headquarters of West Berlin. President Kennedy made his famous 'Ich bin ein Berliner' speech from the balcony here in June 1963.

➕ F9 ✉ Martin-Luther-Strasse 🚉 U-Bahn Rathaus Schöneberg
💵 Free

REICHSTAG

The German parliament building, designed by Paul Wallot in 1884, has had a troubled but colourful history. The inscription on the façade, "For the German people" was added during World War I. In 1933, the Nazis stage-managed a fire in the building as an excuse to do away with the democratic institutions of the Weimar Republic. The

The Reichstag

Reichstag was the focus of the Battle for Berlin in 1945 and by the time Russian soldiers hoisted the Soviet flag the building was a smoking ruin. Fifty years later, restoration was entrusted to British architect Sir Norman Foster. The modern design was completed in 1999 prior to parliament's move from Bonn to Berlin. Although the new design preserved the shell of the building, the interior was gutted to create a new parliamentary chamber. Guided tours of the chamber must be pre-booked but access to the spectacular glass dome and viewing gallery are unrestricted – arrive early or jump the queue by booking a table in the Dachgarten Restaurant (➤ 64).

➕ H5 ✉ Platz der Republik 1 ☎ 22732152 🕐 Daily 8AM–10PM
🚉 S-Bahn Unter den Linden 💵 Free

Parks & Gardens

In the Top 25
🔢 **TIERGARTEN** (➤ 37)

BOTANISCHER GARTEN (BOTANICAL GARDEN)

More than 18,000 varieties of plants and flowers in beautifully landscaped grounds.

➕ Off map to south ✉ Königin-Luise-Strasse 6–8 ☎ 88850027 🕐 Daily May–Oct 9–6; Nov–Apr 9–4 🚇 U-Bahn Rathaus Steglitz 🎫 Moderate

BRITZER GARTEN

Created for the National Garden Show in 1985, the 100-hectare site is a favourite with cyclists, dog owners and families. There is a lake, nature trails and a restaurant.

➕ Off map to south ✉ Sangerhauser Weg 1 ☎ 7009060 🕐 Summer: daily 9–8. Winter: daily 9–4 🚌 Bus 144, 179, 181 🎫 Free

FREIZEITPARK TEGEL

Possibly Berlin's best park – certainly its best for children – with table tennis, rowing, trampolines, volleyball, pedal boats and chess. Pleasure cruisers depart from the Greenwich promenade near by.

➕ Off map to northwest ✉ An der Malche 🚇 U-Bahn Alt-Tegel

The Botanical Garden

GREEN BERLIN

Flying over Berlin, every visitor is struck by the forest and lakes around the city, from Wannsee and the Grunewald in the west to Müggelsee and the Spreewald in the east. The city itself is unusually well provided with municipal parks – on hot Sunday afternoons they are Berliners' favourite spot.

TIERPARK BERLIN-FRIEDRICHSFELDE

One of Berlin's two zoos, located on the east side of the city in grounds that once formed part of Schloss Friedrichsfelde. Concerts and other events are held regularly in the restored palace.

➕ Off map to east ✉ Am Tierpark 125 ☎ 515310 🕐 Daily 9–dark 🚇 U-Bahn Tierpark

TREPTOWER PARK

The largest green space on the eastern side of the city spreads out along the banks of the River Spree. Fairs and other entertainments are often held here.

➕ N8 ✉ Puschkinallee 🚇 S-Bahn Treptower Park

VIKTORIAPARK

Best known for Karl Friedrich Schinkel's *Monument to the Wars of Liberation* (1813–15), this park can be approached from a row of terraces and gardens. There are good views of Berlin from the summit of the park. Children's playground.

➕ H8 ✉ Kreuzbergstrasse 🚇 U-Bahn Platz der Luftbrücke

VOLKSPARK JUNGFERNHEIDE

This park, on the northern edge of Charlottenburg, offers swimming, boat hire, hiking, sports fields and a theatre.

➕ B2 ✉ Saatwinkler Damm 🚇 U-Bahn Siemensdamm

Views

In the Top 25

24 FERNSEHTURM (➤ 47)
18 FRANZÖSISCHER DOM (FRENCH CATHEDRAL ➤ 41)
5 GRUNEWALDTURM (➤ 28)
4 JULIUSTURM, SPANDAU (➤ 27)
14 SIEGESSÄULE ➤ (37)

BLOCKHAUS NIKOLSKOE (➤ 62)

EUROPA-CENTER (➤ 77)

THE FUNKTURM

City wits nicknamed Berlin's broadcasting tower the Langer Lulatsch (Bean Pole). A symbol of German technical prowess at the time that it was first erected, it bears a faint resemblance to the Eiffel Tower in Paris. The restaurant is at a mere 55m, so if you plan to have a meal there, first take the lift up to the 126m-high viewing platform, overlooking the Grunewald forest in one direction and western Berlin in the other.

FUNKTURM

Berlin's broadcasting tower was built between 1924 and 1926 to a design by Heinrich Straumer.
🔲 A6 ✉ Messedamm ☎ Restaurant: 30382996 ⏰ Daily 11:30AM–11PM 🚇 U-Bahn Kaiserdam 🍴 Moderate

'MONT KLAMOTT'

Otherwise known as Grosser Bunkerberg, this is one of the artificial mounds created from rubble cleared from Berlin after World War II. Views are of Prenzlauer Berg and points east.
🔲 M4 ✉ Friedensstrasse 🚇 U-Bahn Strausberger Platz

MÜGGELTURM

A 30m-high tower by the Teufelsee with views of the lake and woodlands of the Müggelsee. There is no lift so be prepared for a climb.
🔲 Off map to southeast ✉ Kleiner Müggelberg ☎ 6541371 ⏰ Daily 9–5 🚌 Bus 169 🍴 Inexpensive

OLYMPIASTADION (OLYMPIC STADIUM)

The 77m-high bell tower (*glockenturm*) of the Olympic Stadium affords views of the Waldbühne (an open-air stadium used for rock concerts), the Grunewald and the River Havel.
🔲 Off map to west ✉ Am Glockenturm Olympische Platz ☎ 3058123 ⏰ Apr–Oct daily 9–6 🚇 S-Bahn Pichelsberg 🍴 Inexpensive

PARK BABELSBERG

From the grounds of this neo-Gothic Schloss built by Karl Friedrich Schinkel in 1833 there are wonderful views across the River Havel towards Potsdam and the Glienicker Bridge.
🔲 Off map to southwest ✉ Allee nach Glienicke 🚌 Bus 691 🍴 Free

The Olympic Stadium

Statues & Monuments

In the Top 25

14 **SIEGESSÄULE (➤ 37)**
19 **STATUE OF FREDERICK THE GREAT (➤ 42)**

MARX AND ENGELS

Unlike the statue of Lenin at Platz der Vereinten Nationen, the monolithic bronze sculptures of Karl Marx and Friedrich Engels will probably survive if only because of their sheer bulk. Just after the Wall came down, a sharp-witted East Berliner spray-painted the plinth with an apology on their behalf: 'We're sorry, it's not our fault – maybe next time things will turn out better.'

HENRY MOORE SCULPTURE, HAUS DER KULTUREN DER WELT

The British artist Henry Moore designed several statues for Berlin. This one, *Large Butterfly*, 'flutters' over a shallow lake outside the Kongresshalle.
🚇 G5 ✉ John-Foster-Dulles-Allee 🚊 S-Bahn Unter den Linden

KLEISTGRAB (KLEIST'S GRAVE)

In a secluded spot in Wannsee is the grave of the Romantic poet Heinrich von Kleist, who committed suicide here with his mistress in 1811.
🚇 Off map to southwest ✉ Bismarckstrasse 🚊 S-Bahn Wannsee

MARX AND ENGELS

The two founders of Communism stand forlorn in a tawdry garden near Alexanderplatz.
🚇 K5 ✉ Rathausstrasse 🚊 U-Bahn Alexanderplatz

MATSCHINSKY-DENNINGHOF SCULPTURE

This sculpture commemorating the 750th anniversary of Berlin's founding was intended to symbolise the schizophrenic existence of what was then still a divided city. It was created by the contemporary artists and married couple, Martin Matschinsky and Brigitte Matschinsky-Denninghof.
🚇 F7 ✉ Tauentzienstrasse 🚊 U-Bahn Wittenbergplatz

Statues of Marx and Engels

MONUMENT TO THE WARS OF LIBERATION (➤ 56)

SCHLOSSBRÜCKE (➤ 54)

SOWJETISCHES EHRENMAL (SOVIET WAR MEMORIAL)

A heavy-handed commemoration of the 20,000 soldiers of the Red Army who died liberating Berlin during World War II.
🚇 H5 ✉ Strasse des 17 Juni 🚊 S-Bahn Unter den Linden

ZILLE

Known affectionately as 'The Poker', this salutes Heinrich Zille (1858–1929) famed for his satirical contributions to *Simplizissimus* magazine.
🚇 L6 ✉ Am Köllnischen Park 🚊 U-Bahn Märkisches Museum

For Children

BABELSBERG FILM STUDIO
Occupying the site of the old UFA studios where Marlene Dietrich began her career, this new theme park, which you visit on a 5- to 6-hour tour, takes a behind-the-scenes look at movie stunts, special effects, pyrotechnics, action scenes, make-up and more.

✚ Off map ✉ Grossbeerenstrasse, Babelsberg ☎ 0331 7212755 ⏰ Daily 10–6 🚉 S-Bahn Griebnitzsee 💷 Expensive

FREIZEITPARK TEGEL (► 56)

GRIPS-THEATER
The show is in German, but there is no language barrier when you watch these puppets.

✚ F5 ✉ Altonaer Strasse 22 ☎ 3914004 ⏰ Mon–Fri noon–6; Sat–Sun noon–5 🚉 U-Bahn Hansaplatz 💷 Expensive

MONBIJOU PARK
This park, near Museums Island, has a playground and a splash pool for toddlers.

✚ J4 ✉ Oranienburger Strasse 🚉 S-Bahn Hackescher Markt

PFAUENINSEL (PEACOCK ISLAND)
Not only peacocks, but a model farm, as well as a nature and bird reserve in a picturesque Wannsee setting. The island is reached by a short ferry ride.

✚ Off map to southwest ✉ Nikolskoer Weg ☎ 80586832 ⏰ Ferry daily 8AM–8PM 🚌 216 (A16) 💷 Inexpensive

ZEISS-GROSSPLANETARIUM
Berlin has three planetariums and observatories. This one gives special monthly shows for children.

✚ M2 ✉ Prenzlauer Allee 80 ☎ 4218450 ⏰ Telephone for show times 🚉 S-Bahn Prenzlauer Allee 💷 Moderate

TRANSPORTATION AND TECHNOLOGY

Deutsches Technikmuseum (The German Technology Museum ► 51) is possibly the most child-orientated museum in Berlin. Its greatest attraction is that most of the displays are hands-on – there is even an experiment room where children can play with computers and other gadgets. The transport section covers everything from ox-carts to vintage cars while technology embraces printing presses, looms, street organs and much else besides.

A shoal of fish on the wall outside the zoo, in Budapester Strasse

THE DAHLEM CHRISTMAS MARKET

This market at Königin-Luise-Strasse 49 offers traditional arts and crafts, games for children and carriage rides to Grunewald.

ZOOLOGISCHER GARTEN (ZOO AND AQUARIUM)
The more conveniently located of Berlin's two zoos.

✚ F6 ✉ Budapester Strasse ⏰ Summer: daily 9–6:30. Winter: daily 9–5 🚉 U- or S-Bahn Zoologischer Garten 💷 Expensive

What's Free

In the Top 25

- ⑧ BATHING IN GRUNEWALD (➤ 28)
- ⑩ DEUTSCHES HISTORISCHES MUSEUM (GERMAN HISTORY MUSEUM ➤ 42)
- ⑩ KAISER-WILHELM-GEDÄCHTNISKIRCHE (KAISER WILHELM MEMORIAL CHURCH ➤ 33)
- ⑩ LISTENING TO BUSKERS ON BREITSCHEIDPLATZ (➤ 33)
- ㉒ ORGAN RECITALS IN BERLIN CATHEDRAL (➤ 45)
- ⑨ SACHSENHAUSEN (➤ 29)
- ⑭ TIERGARTEN (➤ 37)

MONEYSAVERS

Wandering the streets and observing everyday life is the the best free entertainment in town. Most attractions have an admission charge, albeit usually a reasonable one, with reductions for children, students and senior citizens. Some museums offer free admission on Sundays and public holidays. There's no charge at Berlin's many parks (➤ 56) or at the various memorial museums, including the Gedenkstätte Deutscher Widerstand (➤ 60) and the Plötzensee Memorial. Many of the commercial art galleries (➤ 73) are also free.

BIKE RENTAL

Well, *almost* free…Biking is the cheapest way to get around quickly and pleasurably. Hire from **Fahrradstation** at:

➕ K4 ✉ Rosenthalerstrasse 40–1 ☎ 28384848 🚇 S-Bahn Hackescher Markt

➕ J4 ✉ Auguststrasse 29 🚇 S-Bahn Oranienburger Strasse ☎ 28599661

➕ J8 ✉ Bergmannstrasse 9 🚇 U-Bahn Gneisenaustrasse ☎ 2151566

☎ Central information and reservations number: 0180 5108000

Velotaxi is fun, inexpensive and eco-friendly. These three-wheeled bikes have an egg-shaped cabin with seats for two passengers and one rider. Hail them in the street or ☎ 44358990 or 0172 3288888

GEDENKSTÄTTE DEUTSCHER WIDERSTAND (MEMORIAL TO GERMAN RESISTANCE)

The Bendlerblock, focus of the ill-fated conspiracy against Hitler on 20 July 1944, houses an exhibition on opposition to Hitler.

➕ G6 ✉ Stauffenbergstrasse 13 ☎ 26995000 🕐 Mon–Fri 9–6; Thu 9–8; Sat–Sun 10–6 🚇 U-Bahn Kurfürstenstrasse

INTERIOR OF WITTENBERGPLATZ U-BAHN STATION

The 1920s art-deco booking hall has wooden ticket offices, original tiling, and period posters advertising cars and pianos.

➕ F7 ✉ Tauentzienstrasse 🚇 U-Bahn Wittenbergplatz

The Tiergarten, free and right in the middle of Berlin

WANNSEE–KLADOW FERRY

The enjoyable ferry ride from Wannsee to Kladow is inexpensive (free with a *Tageskarte* ➤ 90).

➕ Off map to southwest ✉ Wannsee Pier 🚢 BVG Line F10

BERLIN
where to...

EAT

German Restaurants *62–63*
Other European
 Restaurants *64–65*
International Restaurants *66*
Middle Eastern, Turkish &
 Out-of-Town Restaurants *67*
Cafés *68–69*

SHOP

Department Stores &
 Souvenirs *70*
Boutiques & Designer Clothes *71*
Second-hand & Offbeat *72*
Galleries *73*
Antiques, Glass & Porcelain *74*
Markets & Food Shops *75*
The Best of the Rest *76–77*

BE ENTERTAINED

Theatres & Concerts *78*
Cabaret *79*
Pubs, Bars & Clubs *80–81*
Folk, Jazz & Rock *82*
Sport *83*

STAY

Luxury Hotels *84*
Mid-Range Hotels *85*
Budget Accommodation *86*

German Restaurants

PRICES

The restaurants in this section are in three categories shown by £ signs. Expect to pay per person for a meal, excluding drink:

£	up to 13 Euros; DM25
££	up to 25.5 Euros; DM50
£££	over 25.5 Euros; DM50

TRADITIONAL FARE

In Berlin plates come piled high with the two local staples, meat (usually pork) and potatoes, often accompanied by pickled cabbage (*Sauerkraut*), peas and the ubiquitous pickle. *Buletten* (meatballs) and *Kartoffelpuffer* (savoury potato pancakes) are Berlin specialities. However, young Germans are eschewing this diet and in an increasing number of restaurants the cuisine has been updated to reflect the taste for lighter fare.

ALTES ZOLLHAUS (£££)

An attractive half-timbered former customs house on the Landwehrkanal. Updated German cuisine; fine wines.

➕ K7 ✉ Carl-Herz-Ufer 30 ☎ 6923300 🕒 Tue–Sat 6–1AM 🚇 U-Bahn Prinzenstrasse

AM JULIUSTURM (ZITADELLE) (£££)

You can eat well, if not cheaply, in this tower of a Renaissance fortress. A medieval banqueting experience complete with entertainment.

➕ Off map to west ✉ Juliusturm, Spandau Zitadelle ☎ 3342106 🕒 Tue–Fri 6PM–midnight; Sat–Sun 11AM–midnight 🚇 U-Bahn Zitadelle

BERLINER STUBE (££)

A large restaurant with a terrace specialising in Berlin cooking, including *Eisbein* and *Berliner Leber* (liver).

➕ E7 ✉ Los Angeles Platz 1 ☎ 2127750 🕒 Daily noon–3, 6–11 🚇 U-Bahn Kurfürstendamm

BLOCKHAUS NIKOLSKOE (£££)

A special favourite of Berliners. Situated in secluded woodland, this log cabin was presented in 1818 by Friedrich Wilhelm III to his daughter and her fiancé, the future Czar of Russia, Nicholas I (hence Nikolskoe). Breathtaking views across the Havel from the terrace. Arrive early or book in advance.

➕ Off map to southwest ✉ Nikolskoer Weg 15 ☎ 8052914 🕒 Fri–Wed 10AM–10PM 🚇 S-Bahn Wannsee then bus A16

BORCHARDT (£££)

Fashion-conscious Berliners go to this established restaurant for the fine Sunday brunch.

➕ J5 ✉ Französische Strasse 17 ☎ 2037117 🕒 Daily 11:30AM–1AM 🚇 U-Bahn Französische Strasse

ERMELER HAUS (££)

An 18th-century house with a rococo interior. If the Weinrestaurant is beyond your budget, try the honest German fare in the homely cellar, the Raabe-Diele.

➕ K6 ✉ Märkisches Ufer 10–12 ☎ 2240620 🕒 Tue–Sat 6–11 🚇 U-Bahn Märkisches Museum

FORSTHAUS PAULSBORN (£££)

This stately residence in the Grunewald forest offers coffee, cakes and ice-cream, as well as a full traditional menu.

➕ Off map to southwest ✉ Am Grunewaldsee ☎ 8181910 🕒 Tue–Sun 11AM–11PM 🚇 U-Bahn Oskar-Helene-Heim then bus 115

FUNKTURM (£££)

Updated German cuisine in the radio tower, 55m above Berlin.

➕ A6 ✉ Messedamm 22 ☎ 30382996 🕒 Tue–Sun 11:30AM–11PM 🚇 S-Bahn Witzleben

GUGELHOF (££)

Popular Prenzlauer Berg restaurant with Alsatian specialities – try the trout in Riesling. Reserve ahead.

➕ L3 ✉ Knaackstrasse 37 ☎ 4429229 🕒 Daily 10AM–midnight 🚇 U-Bahn Senefelder

KAFKA (£)

Well-heeled twentysome-
things meet here for
enticing meat and fish
dishes, including
Argentinian roast beef.

🚉 L7 ✉ Oranienstrasse 204
☎ 6122429 🕐 Mon–Sun
11AM–1AM. Breakfast 11AM–3PM
🚇 U-Bahn Görlitzer Banhof

LUTTER & WEGNER (£££)

This historic 19th-century
restaurant on the
Gendarmenmarkt has
Austrian as well as German
cuisine; also a wine bar.

🚉 J5 ✉ Charlottenstrasse 56
☎ 2029541 🕐 Daily
11AM–2AM 🚇 U-Bahn
Hausvogteiplatz

MARJELLCHEN (££)

East Prussian cooking at
good prices. Sorrel soup
and Königsberg
dumplings are specialities.

🚉 C7 ✉ Mommsenstrasse 9
☎ 8832676 🕐 Daily
5PM–midnight. Closed Sun in
summer 🚇 S-Bahn Charlottenburg

RADKE'S GASTHAUS (£££)

Attractive restaurant with
old Berlin cooking. Sunday
brunch noon to 6PM.

🚉 E7 ✉ Marburger Strasse 16
☎ 2134652 🕐 Daily
noon–2AM 🚇 U-Bahn Augsburger
Strasse

RESTAURATION 1900 (££)

This friendly, relaxed
bistro was one of the first
new eateries in Prenzlauer
Berg. Serves good food
and drink.

🚉 L3 ✉ Husemannstrasse 1
☎ 4494052 🕐 Daily
4PM–12:30AM 🚇 U-Bahn
Sennefelder Platz

RÜBEZAHL (££)

Homely Berlin cooking in
attractive surroundings
with a view of the
Müggelsee.

🚉 Off map to southeast ✉ Am
Grossen Müggelsee ☎ 658820
🕐 Daily 6PM–midnight 🚇 S-
Bahn Friedrichshagen then tram 60

SPREE-ATHEN (£££)

This cheerful restaurant in
Charlottenburg takes a
nostalgic look back at the
'good old days' of late
19th- to early 20th-century
Wilhelmine Germany.

🚉 D5 ✉ Leibnizstrasse 60
☎ 3241733 🕐 Mon–Sat 6PM–
midnight 🚇 U-Bahn Deutsche Oper

STÄV (££)

Willi Brandt and other
prominent politicos
enjoyed the Berlin and
Rhineland dishes here.

🚉 H4 ✉ Schiffbauerdamm 8
☎ 2823965 🕐 Daily
11:30AM–late; Sat from 4PM
🚇 U- or S-Bahn Friedrichstrasse

STORCH (££)

A jewel in the crown of
Schöneberg restaurants.
Volker Hauptvogel's
virtuoso variations on
Alsatian dishes are
renowned; the tarte
flambé is a local legend.
No credit cards.

🚉 F8 ✉ Wartburgstrasse 54
☎ 7842059 🕐 Daily 6PM–1AM
🚇 U-Bahn Eisenacher Strasse

VAU (£££)

Currently one of the best
restaurants in the city for
its updated German-
Austrian cuisine.

🚉 J5 ✉ Jägerstrasse 54–55
☎ 2029730 🕐 Mon–Sat
noon–2:30, 6–11 🚇 U-Bahn
Französische Strasse

GERMAN WINES

Roman conquerors began
growing wine in Germany
more than 2,000 years ago.
Today the country is divided
into 13 distinct wine-growing
regions, mainly along the
Rhine and Moselle river
valleys. Nearly all the wine is
white, relying heavily on the
Müller-Thurgau and Riesling
grapes. Red wines are not
generally held in high esteem
and are not usually consumed
locally. As a major wine
producer, Germany offers a
diverse range from earthy and
dry to mellow and sweet.
German wine laws require
strict quality controls.

Other European Restaurants

BAMBERGER REITER

German food lovers travel far to visit Franz Raneburger's famous restaurant. Raneburger, Austrian by birth, describes his cooking as Austro-Prussian. However, his culinary creations are by no means confined to the territories of these historic rivals – even France is represented on the menu. The goose-liver tarts are not to be missed.

FRENCH

ALT LUXEMBURG (£££)
One of the best restaurants in the city. Chef Karl Wannemacher has a way with herbs.
⊞ C6 ⊠ Windscheidstrasse 31 ☎ 3238730 ⊙ Tue–Sat 7PM–11PM ⊚ U-Bahn Sophie-Charlotten-Platz

BOVRIL (£££)
Bistro with fresh, beautifully presented, French-German food. Popular with businessmen and literati.
⊞ E7 ⊠ Ku'damm 184 ☎ 8818461 ⊙ Mon–Sat noon–2AM ⊚ U-Bahn Uhlandstrasse

COUR CARRÉE (££)
Fin-de-siècle Berlin lives on in this fine restaurant. No credit cards.
⊞ D6 ⊠ Savignyplatz 5 ☎ 3125238 ⊙ Daily noon–2AM ⊚ S-Bahn Savignyplatz

DACHGARTEN (£££)
Updated dishes such as breast of guinea fowl with lobster and morel are served on the roof-terrace of the parliament building. Reservations are a must.
⊞ H5 ⊠ Platz der Republik ☎ 22629933 ⊙ Daily 8AM–11PM ⊚ S-Bahn Unter den Linden

FRANZÖSISCHER HOF (£££)
Elegant, with views of the Gendarmenmarkt and Schinkel's magnificent concert hall.
⊞ J5 ⊠ Jägerstrasse 56 ☎ 2043570 ⊙ Daily 11AM–midnight ⊚ U-Bahn Französische Strasse

LE CANARD (£££)
One of the delights of Savignyplatz. Boisterous Le Canard specialises in southern French cuisine. Music.
⊞ D7 ⊠ Knesebeckstrasse 88 ☎ 3122645 ⊙ Mon–Sat 5PM–midnight ⊚ S-Bahn Savignyplatz

GREEK

AKROPOLIS ATHEN (££)
Friendly Greek taverna with popular summer terrace.
⊞ Off map to south ⊠ Burgenmeisterstrasse 21 (Tempelhof) ☎ 7514923 ⊙ Daily 5PM–midnight; Sun noon–midnight ⊚ U-Bahn Kaiserin-Augusta Strasse

ITALIAN

BAR CENTRALE (££)
Stylish young Berliners crowd the bar and tables out on the pavement. The Italian food is beautifully presented, service is courteous and newspaper vendors drop in with early copies of tomorrow's edition. Round off your meal with a grappa.
⊞ H8 ⊠ Yorckstrasse 82 ☎ 7862989 ⊙ Daily 6PM–3AM ⊚ U- or S-Bahn Yorckstrasse

CANDELA (££)
Busy but relaxed Schöneberg restaurant with friendly staff and wholesome Italian cooking. Reserve for weekends.
⊞ F8 ⊠ Grunewaldstrasse 81 ☎ 7821409 ⊙ Daily 5PM–1AM ⊚ U-Bahn Eisenacher Strasse

DON CAMILLO (£££)

Prices reflect the esteem in which this Italian restaurant is held. Near Schloss Charlottenburg.

➕ C5 ✉ Schlossstrasse 7 ☎ 3223572 🕐 Mon–Sat 6–10:30PM 🚇 U-Bahn Sophie-Charlotten-Platz

TRATTORIA À MUNTAGNOLA (£££)

The celebrated cook, Mamma Angela, draws on the recipes of Muntagnola in southern Italy.

➕ F7 ✉ Fuggerstrasse 27 ☎ 2116642 🕐 Daily noon–midnight 🚇 U-Bahn Nollendorfplatz

TRATTORIA LAPPEGGI (££)

Easy-going Italian restaurant in Prenzlauer Berg. Inventive pasta.

➕ L3 ✉ Kollwitzstrasse 56 ☎ 4426347 🕐 Daily noon–midnight 🚇 U-Bahn Senerfelderplatz

MIXED EUROPEAN

BAMBERGER REITER (£££)

Reservations are essential at this outstanding restaurant (► 64 panel).

➕ E7 ✉ Regensburgerstrasse 7 ☎ 2184282 🕐 Tue–Sat 6PM–1AM 🚇 U-Bahn Spichernstrasse

REINHARD'S (££)

This busy, modern bistro is splendidly located in the sedate rococo Nikolai-viertel, not far from Alexanderplatz.

➕ K5 ✉ Poststrasse 28 ☎ 2425295 🕐 Sun–Thu 9AM–midnight; Fri–Sat 9AM–1AM 🚇 U- or S-Bahn Alexanderplatz

PORTUGUESE

CARAVELA (£)

Wonderful grilled fish in a southern suburb. Loyal following.

➕ Off map to south ✉ Dickhardstrasse 27 ☎ 8522660 🕐 Daily noon–midnight 🚇 U-Bahn Walther-Schreiber-Platz

LUSIADA (££)

Fish dishes take pride of place in this laid-back Portuguese restaurant on Berlin's most famous avenue.

➕ D7 ✉ Ku'damm 132a ☎ 8915869 🕐 Daily 5PM–4AM 🚇 U-Bahn Uhlandstrasse

RUSSIAN

PASTERNAK (££)

Marina Lehmann's lovely restaurant has a literary theme. Book ahead.

➕ L3 ✉ Knaackstrasse 24 ☎ 4413399 🕐 Mon–Sat noon–2AM; Sun 10AM–2AM 🚇 U-Bahn Senefelderplatz

SPANISH

CARPE DIEM (££)

Large, lively and central. Tables are set up in the shadows of the S-Bahn arches in summer. No credit cards.

➕ D6 ✉ Savigny Passage, Arch 576–7 ☎ 3132728 🕐 Mon–Sat noon–1AM 🚇 S-Bahn Savignyplatz

LA PALOMA (££)

Bright and airy spot for paella, sangria and other Iberian fare.

➕ M7 ✉ Skalitzerstrasse 54 ☎ 6182450 🕐 Daily 5PM–midnight 🚇 U-Bahn Görlitzer Banhof

---

AT THE WÜRSTCHENBUDE

Sausage stands (*Würstchenbudes*) and snack bars (*Schnellimbiss*) are popular in Germany with people who want to have a quick bite to eat on the run. These stands usually offer *Thüringer Bratwurst* (grilled sausage), the spicier *Krakauer* and *Frankfurter Bockwurst*. These are normally served in a bread roll with mustard. Bigger stands offer a choice of french fries, potato salad and *Sauerkraut* (pickled cabbage). Other snacks include hamburger meat balls, served hot or cold. These are called *Buletten* in Berlin or *Frikadellen* elsewhere.

International Restaurants

HEALTH ON THE MENU

Recent food scares in Germany and abroad may prompt health-conscious Germans to change their eating habits. Traditionally veal and pork have been part of their staple diet but poultry, fish and non-meat dishes are gaining popularity both at home and in restaurants. The numbers of Oriental and vegetarian establishments have been climbing as well.

CHINESE

HO LIN WAH (£££)

Authentic Chinese dishes in an opulent but intimate former embassy.

🏠 D7 ✉ Ku'damm 218
☎ 8821171 🕐 Daily
noon–midnight 🚇 U-Bahn
Uhlandstrasse

INDIAN

INDIA (££)

Reasonably priced meat and vegetarian dishes.

🏠 J8 ✉ Bergmannstrasse 100
☎ 6926976 🕐 Daily
noon–midnight 🚇 U-Bahn
Gneisenaustrasse

MAHARADSCHA (£££)

A classic Indian restaurant in the heart of the city. Go for the lamb and chicken curries or the vegetarian dishes – or perhaps try the *palak panir* (cream cheese with spinach).

🏠 F7 ✉ Fuggerstrasse 21
☎ 2138826 🕐 Daily
noon–midnight 🚇 U-Bahn
Nollendorfplatz

INDONESIAN

TUK-TUK (££)

Indonesian paintings, woodcarvings and gamelan music enliven this Schöneberg restaurant. Vegetarian dishes are a speciality.

🏠 G8 ✉ Grossgörschenstrasse 2 ☎ 7811588 🕐 Daily
5:30PM–1AM 🚇 U- or S-Bahn
Yorckstrasse

JAPANESE

SAPPORO-KAN (£££)

Practised purveyors of sushi and other Japanese delicacies. Very popular so book ahead.

🏠 D7 ✉ Schlüterstrasse 52
☎ 8812973 🕐 Mon–Sat
noon–2PM, 6PM–midnight;
Sun 6PM–midnight 🚇 S-Bahn
Savignyplatz

KOREAN

KWANG JU GRILL (£)

The South Korean chef serves up huge portions of sweet and sour chicken, pork ribs and more.

🏠 D8 ✉ Emser Strasse 24
☎ 8839794 🕐 Daily
noon–midnight; Fri, Sat till 2AM
🚇 U-Bahn Hohenzollernplatz

THAI

MAI PHAI (££)

Warm and atmospheric restaurant with rattan chairs, exotic plants and Thai music. Good value.

🏠 Off map to south
✉ Feuerbachstrasse 16, Steglitz
☎ 7922845 🕐 Mon
5PM–midnight; Tue–Sun
noon–midnight 🚇 U-Bahn
Feuerbachstrasse

MAO THAI (££)

An intimate cellar restaurant. Try the pineapple and coconut filled with shrimp.

🏠 L3 ✉ Wörther Strasse 30
☎ 4419261 🕐 Daily
noon–2:30, 6–11:30
🚇 U-Bahn Senefelderplatz

VEGETARIAN

THÜRNAGEL (££)

A no-frills place serving imaginative vegetarian dishes. No credit cards.

🏠 J8 ✉ Gneisenaustrasse 57
☎ 6914800 🕐 Daily
6–midnight 🚇 U-Bahn
Gneisenaustrasse

Middle Eastern, Turkish & Out-of-Town Restaurants

MIDDLE EASTERN

BAGDAD (££)

One of Kreuzberg's most popular haunts. The garden is a plus.

➕ N7 ✉ Schlesische Strasse 2 ☎ 6126962 🕐 Daily 11:30AM–midnight 🚇 U-Bahn Schlesisches Tor

DER ÄGYPTER (££)

One of the few Middle Eastern restaurants in this part of town. Good vegetarian selection.

➕ C6 ✉ Kantstrasse 26 ☎ 3139230 🕐 Daily 5PM–1AM 🚇 U-Bahn Wilmersdorfer Strasse

TURKISH

FOYER (£££)

Classy Anatolian cooking in the centre of town. Try the spicy meatballs with feta cheese filling or the aromatic lamb chops.

➕ E6 ✉ Uhlandstrasse 28 ☎ 8814268 🕐 Daily noon–3, 6–midnight 🚇 U-Bahn Uhlandstrasse

HIT IT (££)

Traditional spicy meat and vegetarian dishes are carefully prepared by an inventive chef.

➕ B5 ✉ Knobelsdorffstrasse 35 ☎ 3224557 🕐 Daily noon–midnight 🚇 U-Bahn Sophie-Charlotte-Platz

ISTANBUL (££)

This well-known establishment is not cheap but the food is authentic.

➕ D7 ✉ Knesebeckstrasse 77 ☎ 8832777 🕐 Daily noon–midnight 🚇 S-Bahn Savignyplatz

MERHABA (££)

No frills – where the local Turkish community eats.

➕ K8 ✉ Hasenheide 39 ☎ 6921713 🕐 Mon–Sat 4PM–midnight 🚇 U-Bahn Südstern

OUT-OF-TOWN

DER KLOSTERKELLER (£££)

A historic restaurant, near the Dutch Quarter in Potsdam, with traditional Prussian food and entertainment.

➕ Off map ✉ Friedrich-Ebert-Strasse 94 ☎ (0331) 291218 🕐 Daily noon–midnight 🚇 S-Bahn Potsdam Stadt

IGEL (££)

A friendly hotel-restaurant in north Berlin with views of the Tegeler See and the River Havel.

➕ Off map to north-east ✉ Friederikestrasse 20 ☎ 4367980 🕐 Daily 8AM–11PM 🚇 U-Bahn Alt Tegel then bus 222

LORETTA AM WANNSEE (££)

A large garden restaurant, next door to the harbour and overlooking Wannsee lake. Near the S-Bahn. Grills and fish.

➕ Off map ✉ Kronprinzessinnenweg 260 ☎ 8035156 🕐 Daily 9AM–1AM 🚇 S-Bahn Wannsee

RATSKELLER (££)

A welcoming cellar restaurant in Babelsberg's Old Town Hall serving traditional German food.

➕ Off map ✉ Karl Liebknecht-Strasse 135 ☎ (0331) 707426 🕐 Daily 11:30AM–midnight 🚇 S-Bahn Babelsberg

LITTLE ISTANBUL

Kreuzberg, a traditional working-class district near the centre of Berlin, has the largest Turkish community outside Istanbul. In the exotic neighbourhoods of Kottbusser Tor and Schlesisches Tor dozens of restaurants offer inexpensive and authentic Anatolian cuisine.

Cafés

CAFÉS IN RETREAT

Rising rents on fashionable Kurfürstendamm have forced Berlin's two most famous cafés, Kranzler and Möhring, to close their large pavement-café premises. For many decades these had been popular meeting places. Café Kranzler has now re-opened as a second-floor café and bistro, after yielding the street-level space below to a fashion shop. Café Möhring survives at smaller premises near Gendarmenmarkt in eastern Berlin.

AM STADTTOR (£)

Baguettes, snacks, and more substantial meals are all available from this café near Potsdam's Brandenburg Gate.

➕ Off map ✉ Brandenburger Strasse 1–3, Potsdam ☎ 0331 291791 🕐 Mon–Fri 9AM–11PM; Sun 12 noon–11PM 🚇 S-Bahn Potsdam Hauptbahnhof

BARCOMI'S DELI (£)

Friendly courtyard deli with an enticing range of American snacks – everything from bagels to chocolate cake.

➕ K4 ✉ Sophienstrasse 21 ☎ 29598363 🕐 Mon–Sat 9AM–10PM; Sun from 10AM 🚇 S-Bahn Hackescher Markt

CAFÉ AEDES (££)

A trendy spot for those who want to see and be seen. There is an art gallery too.

➕ D6 ✉ Savigny Passage, Arch 599 ☎ 3125504 🕐 Daily 9AM–midnight 🚇 S-Bahn Savignyplatz

CAFÉ BLEIBTREU (£)

This espresso bar, popular with young trendies, is convenient to Savignyplatz. Buffet breakfast Sat and Sun 9:30AM–3:30PM.

➕ D6 ✉ Bleibtreustrasse 31 ☎ 884740 🕐 Daily 9:30AM–1AM 🚇 S-Bahn Savignyplatz

CAFÉ EINSTEIN (££)

Traditional Viennese-style coffee house trying to re-create a pre-war Berlin café atmosphere. There are newspapers and a garden, but prices are steep.

➕ F7 ✉ Kurfürstenstrasse 58 ☎ 2615096 🕐 Daily till 2AM 🚇 U-Bahn Kurfürstenstrasse

CAFÉ KRANZLER (££)

The traditional Berlin café is an Austrian import – Johann Georg Kranzler opened his first coffee shop in 1835. Café Kranzler now overlooks the Ku'damm from its second-floor location. An intriguing selection of cakes, pastries and ice creams include local favourites such as *Quark-kirschkuchen* (cheesecake with cherries) and *Mokkatorte* (coffee cake).

➕ D7 ✉ Ku'damm 18 ☎ 882820 🕐 Daily 8AM–midnight 🚇 U-Bahn Uhlandstrasse

CAFÉ M (££)

One of Schöneberg's most popular late-night haunts, with non-stop breakfasts. No frills, but plenty of atmosphere.

➕ F8 ✉ Goltzstrasse 33 ☎ 2167092 🕐 Daily 9AM–2AM 🚇 U-Bahn Nollendorfplatz

CAFÉ MÖHRING (££)

Quiet and formal *Konditorei* perfect for morning coffee. Wide variety of delicious *Torten* and ice cream.

➕ J5 ✉ Charlottenstrasse 55 ☎ 203092240 🕐 Daily 8AM–midnight 🚇 U-Bahn Französische Strasse

CAFÉ OREN (£)

Light and airy café-restaurant near the Synagogue. An exotic mix of Israeli and Middle Eastern dishes; red wine from the Golan Heights.

➕ J4 ✉ Oranienburger Strasse 28 ☎ 2828228 🕐 Daily 10AM–1AM 🚇 S-Bahn Hackescher Markt

CAFÉ ÜBERSEE (£)
Busy into the early hours, this attractive Kreuzberg café serves breakfast until 4PM daily.

➕ L7   ✉ Paul-Lincke-Ufer 44
☎ 6188765   🕐 Daily 9AM–2AM   🚇 U-Bahn Kottbusser Tor

FRESSCO (£)
Stylish *Imbisshalle* (snack bar) serving vegetarian as well as meaty snacks. Opposite Tacheles.

➕ J4   ✉ Oranienburger Strasse 48–9   ☎ 2829647
🕐 Daily 10AM –1AM
🚇 U-Bahn Oranienburger Tor

OPERNCAFÉ (£)
Redolent of old Berlin, this palatial café with an expensive restaurant upstairs is next to the Staatsoper.

➕ J5   ✉ Unter den Linden 5
☎ 202683   🕐 Daily 8:30AM–midnight   🚇 U-Bahn Französische Strasse

RESTAURANT EOSANDER (££)
Old sepia photographs line the walls of this turn-of-the-century café across from Schloss Charlottenburg. Children's menu.

➕ C5   ✉ Spandauer Damm 3–5   ☎ 3423037   🕐 Mon–Sat 9AM–midnight; Sun 9AM–10PM
🚇 U-Bahn Richard-Wagner-Platz

SCHWARZES CAFÉ (££)
Nightclubbers on their way home meet businesspeople setting off for work.

➕ D6   ✉ Kantstrasse 148
☎ 3138038   🕐 Daily from 5AM
🚇 S-Bahn Savignyplatz

SOUP-KULTUR (£)
The last word in snacks plus a selection of the world's tastiest soups.

➕ D7   ✉ Kufürstendamm 224
☎ 88629282   🕐 Sun–Fri 11AM–8PM; Sat 11AM–4PM   🚇 U-Bahn Uhlandstrasse

TADSCHIKISCHE TEESTUBE (££)
A strictly no-smoking tea house where footsore visitors to the Mitte can kick off their shoes and loll on Tadzhik divans.

➕ J5   ✉ In Palais am Festungsgraben (behind the Neue Wache)   ☎ 2010693
🕐 Mon–Fri 5PM–midnight; Sat–Sun 3PM–midnight   🚌 Bus 100, 157

TIM'S CANADIAN DELI (£)
Busy café convenient to the weekend market on Winterfeldtplatz. Brownies and muffins.

➕ F7   ✉ Maassenstrasse 14
☎ 21756960   🕐 Mon–Sat 8AM–midnight; Sun from 9AM
🚇 U-Bahn Nollendorfplatz

YORCKSCHLÖSSCHEN (£)
This busy locals' café has an extensive breakfast menu.

➕ J8   ✉ Yorckstrasse 15
☎ 2158070   🕐 Daily 9AM–late   🚇 U-Bahn Mehringdamm

ZUM NUSSBAUM (£)
A traditional Berlin *Gasthaus* located near Fischerinsel in Nikolaiviertal.

➕ K5   ✉ Am Nussbaum 3
☎ 2423095   🕐 Daily noon–2AM   🚇 U- or S-Bahn Alexanderplatz

BREAKFAST IN BERLIN

For Berliners, breakfast is a way of life. You can, it seems, take the meal at any time of the day, and you can spend as long over it as you like. Ham and eggs, sausage, cheese, muesli, pumpernickel and even cakes may be on the agenda.

Department Stores & Souvenirs

SHOPPING HOURS

Most shops open between 9AM and 10AM and close at 6PM or 6:30PM. Many are closed on Saturday afternoon.

DEUTSCHER BUNDESTAG SHOP

Souvenirs and political memorabilia, including tankards, Berlin Wall maps, mugs, military caps, medals and keyrings.

➕ J5 ✉ Unter den Linden 69b ☎ 22679821 🚈 S-Bahn Unter den Linden

GALERIES LAFAYETTE

Branch of the Parisian shopping mecca. An architectural treat too, with its impressive curved glass wall, curved roof and two huge glass cones inside.

➕ J5 ✉ Französische Strasse 2 ☎ 209480 🕐 Mon–Fri 9:30AM–8PM; Sat 9AM–4PM 🚈 U-Bahn Französische Strasse

GIPSFORMEREI

Ideal for last-minute present buyers, the museum shop at Schloss Charlottenburg specialises in plaster casts of well known museum exhibits such as the famous bust of Queen Nefertiti.

➕ B5 ✉ Sophie-Charlotten-Strasse 17–18 ☎ 3217011 🕐 Closed Sat 🚈 U-Bahn Sophie-Charlotten-Platz

INFORMATION OFFICE, BERLIN TOURISMUS MARKETING

Excellent selection of typical Berlin souvenirs.

➕ E6 ✉ Budapester Strasse 45 (also Brandenburg Gate) ☎ 250025 🕐 Mon–Sat 8AM–10PM; Sun 9AM–9PM 🚈 U- or S-Bahn Zoologischer Garten

KADEWE (KAUFHAUS DES WESTENS)

The second largest department store in the world (after Harrods of London), stocking some 250,000 items. The Food Hall is a must (▶ 75).

➕ F7 ✉ Tauentzienstrasse 21–4 ☎ 21210 🚈 U-Bahn Wittenbergplatz

KAUFHOF

This western department store occupies the premises of an outmoded East German predecessor.

➕ L4 ✉ Alexanderplatz ☎ 247430 🚈 U- or S-Bahn Alexanderplatz

POTSDAMER PLATZ ARKADEN

The architecturally noteworthy Renzo Piano mall has 120 shops, plus cafés and restaurants.

➕ H6 ✉ Potsdamer Platz 🚈 U- or S-Bahn Potsdamer Platz

QUELLE

Look out for all the usual household items in this department store in Wedding.

➕ G2 ✉ Müller Strasse 153 ☎ 4650980 🚈 U-Bahn Leopoldplatz

SCENARIO

A quirky shop selling wacky gifts and souvenirs, leather, stationery, cards and jewellery.

➕ D6 ✉ Savigny Passage, Arch 602 ☎ 3129199 🚈 S-Bahn Savignyplatz

WERTHEIM

Traditional department store selling a good range of T-shirts, mugs and other gifts bearing the Berlin logo. Located near the Kaiser-Wilhelm-Gedächtniskirche.

➕ E7 ✉ Ku'damm 231 ☎ 880030 🚈 U-Bahn Kurfürstendamm

Boutiques & Designer Clothes

BAGAGE

This Kreuzberg shop sells bags of all shapes, sizes and colours – everything from handbags and satchels to rucksacks and travel bags.
➕ J8 ✉ Bergmannstrasse 13 ☎ 6939816 🚇 U-Bahn Gneisenaustrasse

BLEIBGRÜN

Purveyors of designer shoes and bags with sought-after labels.
➕ D7 ✉ Bleibtreustrasse 27 ☎ 8850080 🚇 U-Bahn Uhlandstrasse

EISDIELER

A showcase for young Berlin designers.
➕ J4 ✉ Auguststrasse 74 🚇 U-Bahn Oranienburger Tor

GIANNI VERSACE

Berlin's outlet for the latest creations from the famous Italian designer's fashion house.
➕ D7 ✉ Kurfürstendamm 185 ☎ 8857460 🚇 U-Bahn Uhlandstrasse

HELLMANN POUR ELLE

One of a chain of five shops owned by Patrick Hellmann. Fashion items are aimed at sophisticated, well-heeled shoppers. Gaultier and Calvin Klein are represented here.
➕ E7 ✉ Fasanenstrasse 26 ☎ 8824201 🚇 U-Bahn Uhlandstrasse

JIL SANDER

Understated but eye-catching fashions from the celebrity German designer.
➕ D7 ✉ Kurfürstendamm 185 ☎ 8867020 🚇 U-Bahn Uhlandstrasse

KOSTÜMHAUS

The sound of sewing machines in the background is proof that the ladieswear is tailored on the premises.
➕ K4 ✉ Rosenthaler Strasse 40–41 ☎ 2827018 🚇 S-Bahn Hackescher Markt

KRAMBERG

Top designer names are represented in this store, which appeals to fashion sophisticates of both sexes.
➕ D7 ✉ Ku'damm 56–7 ☎ 3279010 🚇 U-Bahn Adenauerplatz

LISA D

Popular boutique in the Hackesche Höfe with its own stylish creations.
➕ K4 ✉ Rosenthaler Strasse 40–41 ☎ 2829061 🚇 S-Bahn Hackescher Markt

MIKES LADEN

International fashions for men and women.
➕ E7 ✉ Nürnberger Strasse 50–56 ☎ 2182020 🚇 U-Bahn Augsburger Strasse

MOLOTOW

Newer Berlin designers sell imaginative clothing here. The styles for men and women range from classical to more modern designs.
➕ J8 ✉ Gneisenastrasse 112 ☎ 6930818 🚇 U-Bahn Mehringdamm

NIX

Chic clothing for men, women and children. The shop is located in Mitte.
➕ J4 ✉ Auguststrasse 86 ☎ 2818044 🚇 U-Bahn Oranienburger Tor

CITY ORIGINALS

Where fashion is concerned, Berlin is not a city you would mention in the same breath as Paris, London, or Milan, but Berliners are as style-conscious as the inhabitants of any other cosmopolitan city. The boutiques off the Ku'damm – for example in Knesebeckstrasse, Uhlandstrasse or Pariserstrasse – include some of the city's own fashion houses, promoting the creations of Patrick Hellmann, Jutta Meierling and others.

Second-hand & Offbeat

THE ALTERNATIVE SCENE

Berlin's chic cosmopolitan image is constantly being undermined by a brazenly nonconformist alternative with roots in the 1960s. There is plenty of evidence of the latter in the remarkable variety of stores specialising in second-hand and offbeat clothing and jewellery. You can have great fun inspecting the wares. A good starting point is the Garage, which sells used clothes by the kilo. The more discerning should sample Kaufhaus Schrill.

AVE MARIA

Devotional statues and other kitschy items compete for your attention with clothing for men, women and children.
🕇 G7 ✉ Potsdamer Strasse 75 ☎ 2621211 🚇 U-Bahn Kurfürstenstrasse

GARAGE

Clothes are sold by weight in this large warehouse near Nollendorfplatz U-Bahn station. It claims to be Europe's biggest second-hand store.
🕇 F7 ✉ Ahornstrasse 2 ☎ 2112760 🚇 U-Bahn Nollendorfplatz

KANT STORE

Cowboy boots, leather leggings and other items for shoppers with unconventional tastes.
🕇 D6 ✉ Kantstrasse 33 ☎ 3135640 🚇 S-Bahn Savignyplatz

KAUFHAUS SCHRILL

Showy accessories – everything from hats and gloves to ties and loud jewellery. The roll-call of former patrons is said to include Sylvester Stallone.
🕇 D6 ✉ Bleibtreustrasse 46 ☎ 8824048 🚇 S-Bahn Savignyplatz

KNOPF-PAUL

The ingenious owner of this Kreuzberg shop makes buttons out of everything – even plum stones and typewriter keys.
🕇 J8 ✉ Zossener Strasse 10 ☎ 6921212 🚇 U-Bahn Gneisenaustrasse

MADE IN BERLIN

Second-hand clothes of quality, including 1920s cocktail dresses and tuxedos from the 1950s.
🕇 G8 ✉ Potsdamer Strasse 106 ☎ 2622431 🚇 U-Bahn Kurfürstenstrasse

RIO

Sophisticated costume jewellery by Lagerfeld and Montana is the speciality at this exclusive store near Savignyplatz.
🕇 D6 ✉ Bleibtreustrasse 52 ☎ 3133152 🚇 S-Bahn Savignyplatz

SCHÖNHAUSER

Where else but in former East Berlin would you expect to find outmoded gadgets from the 1970s and 1980s—blenders, pop-up toasters, lamps and furniture.
🕇 K4 ✉ Neue Schönhauser Strasse 18 ☎ 2811704 🚇 U-Bahn Hackescher Markt

SCHWARZE MODE

For shoppers with a taste for latex and leather. The name translates as 'black fashion'.
🕇 F8 ✉ Grunewaldstrasse 91 ☎ 7845922 🚇 U-Bahn Eisenacher Strasse

UP ARTS

Ward off evil spirits with African wood carvings, charms, amulets, bracelets and face masks.
🕇 F7 ✉ Goltzstrasse 12 ☎ 2169021 🚇 U-Bahn Nollendorfplatz

WAAHNSINN BERLIN

Fashion and oddities from the 1920s to the 1970s including handspun tops from Bali.
🕇 K5 ✉ Neue Promenada 3 ☎ 2820029 🚇 S-Bahn Hackescher Markt

Galleries

DAAD
Avant-garde and modern art.

✚ F5 ✉ Kurfürstenstrasse 58
☎ 2022080 🕐 Daily
12:30PM–7PM 🚌 Bus 100

GALERIE BREMER
An established gallery that exhibits the work of contemporary German artists, including newcomers. A bar by architect Hans Scharoun opens in the evenings.

✚ E7 ✉ Fasanenstrasse 37
☎ 8814908 🕐 Tue–Fri
noon–6 🚇 U-Bahn
Uhlandstrasse

GALERIE BRUSBERG
The place to come for Dada and surrealist art, plus the occasional Picasso and Mirò.

✚ E7 ✉ Ku'damm 213
☎ 8827682 🕐 Tue–Fri
10–6:30; Sat 10–2 🚇 U-Bahn
Uhlandstrasse

GALERIA GROTH
Among the pieces exhibited here are reproductions of pre-Columbian objects from Bogotá.

✚ E7 ✉ Uhlandstrasse 170
(passage) ☎ 8818161
🚇 U-Bahn Uhlandstrasse

GALERIE
PELS-LEUSDEN
International art of the 19th and 20th centuries, displayed in the beautiful former home of turn-of-the-20th-century architect Hans Grisebach.

✚ E7 ✉ Fasanenstrasse 25
☎ 8859150 🕐 Mon–Fri
10–6:30; Sat 10–2
🚇 U-Bahn Uhlandstrasse

GALERIE
WOHNMASCHINE
Promotes the work of up-and-coming but impoverished artists.

✚ J4 ✉ Tucholskystrasse 34
☎ 30872015 🕐 Tue, Wed, Fri,
Sat 2–7; Thu 5–9 🚇 S-Bahn
Oranienburger Strasse

HACKESCHE HÖFE
Now smartened up, these historic courtyards remain at the heart of Berlin's contemporary art scene with their galleries, workshops and cafés.

✚ K4 ✉ Rosenthaler Strasse
☎ No phone 🚇 S-Bahn
Hackescher Markt

KUNST-WERKE BERLIN
Experimental and avant-garde art in one of Auguststrasse's new galleries.

✚ J4 ✉ Auguststrasse 69
☎ 2817325 🚇 S-Bahn
Oranienburger Strasse

SOPHIE GIPS HÖFE
This converted factory is now a centre for contemporary arts with studios, galleries and cafés. Near Hackesche Höfe (above).

✚ K4 ✉ Sophienstrasse 21
☎ 2836580 🕐 Tue–Sat
noon–6PM 🚇 S-Bahn
Hackescher Markt

TACHELES
Splendidly dilapidated Tacheles remains a centre of experimental and offbeat art.

✚ J4 ✉ Oranienburger Strasse
54–56 ☎ 2826185
🚇 S-Bahn Oranienburger Strasse

ART OF ALL KINDS

Artists generally divide into two groups: the up-and-coming and those who have already made it. The exclusive private galleries around Fasanenstrasse promote the work of established German artists while also exhibiting some of the best in international modern art. The other side of the coin is the collection of crumbling ateliers and studios in Kreuzberg and the Scheunenviertel, where the undiscovered, neglected and uncompromising show off their work.

Antiques, Glass & Porcelain

ROYAL PORCELAIN

Berlin's historic association with porcelain dates from 1763 when Frederick the Great founded the Königliche Porzellan Manufaktor (Royal Porcelain Factory, or KPM). It is still going strong today. The firm's principal outlet (with showroom) is on the Ku'damm, but the famous KPM hallmark crops up all over the city. The best place to see the historic pieces is the Belvedere at Schloss Charlottenburg (➤ 31).

ANTIQUE LAMPEN

The name of this Charlottenburg emporium says it all. Old lamps, including genuine art-deco and Victorian models, restored to pristine condition, are available – at a price.

➕ C7 ✉ Gervinusstrasse 15
☎ 3233427 🚇 S-Bahn Charlottenburg

ART 1900

Specialist dealers in Jugendstil and art deco – pictures, porcelain, furniture, jewellery and lamps.

➕ E7 ✉ Kurfürstendamm 53
☎ 8815627 🚇 U-Bahn Kurfürstendamm

ART & INDUSTRY

Furniture, lamps and accessories in Bauhaus and other functionalist styles. Also watches.

➕ D7 ✉ Bleibtreustrasse 40
☎ 8834946 🚇 S-Bahn Savignyplatz

GEDAN

This porcelain specialist deals in the world's top designers, including Rosenthal, Wedgewood and Nachtmann.

➕ Off map to south
✉ Hermanstrasse 38
☎ 6289240 🚇 U- or S-Bahn Hermanstrasse

GLÄSER JAN HINRICHS

A must if you are looking for glassware and don't want to pay through the nose. Prices are more affordable than most and the selection is good.

➕ D7 ✉ Knesebeckstrasse 13–14 ☎ 3131037
🚇 S-Bahn Savignyplatz

KPM

Quality porcelain bearing the renowned KPM hallmark (see panel).

➕ C7 ✉ Ku'damm 26a
☎ 8867210 🚇 U-Bahn Adenauerplatz

MEISSENER PORZELLAN

Figurines and other decorative items made of Meissen porcelain.

➕ D7 ✉ Kurfürstendamm 214 ☎ 2679028 🚇 U-Bahn Uhlandstrasse

Also at:

➕ J5 ✉ Unter den Linden 39B
☎ 8819158 🚌 Bus 100

RUSSISCHE SAMOWARE

Beautiful antique Russian Samovars dating back to before the Revolution.

➕ E7 ✉ Marburger Strasse 5
☎ 211 3666 🚇 U-Bahn Augsburger Strasse

SEIDEL UND SOHN

Antiques shop specialising in Biedermeier furniture and household items.

➕ F8 ✉ Eisenacher Strasse 13
☎ 2161850 🚇 U-Bahn Eisenacher Strasse

WILHELM WEIK

Furniture, paintings and porcelain of the 18th–19th centuries. In the centre of Berlin's antique district.

➕ F7 ✉ Eisenacher Strasse 10
☎ 6062837 🚇 U-Bahn Viktoria-Luise-Platz

YOKOHAMA HAUS

The Meissen porcelain on sale here is a long-time rival of the famous KPM of Berlin.

➕ E7 ✉ Keithstrasse 10
☎ 2183135 🚇 U-Bahn Wittenbergplatz

Markets & Food Shops

ANTIK UND FLOHMARKT
Affordable antiques and bric-à-brac beneath the arches of Friedrichstrasse station.

➕ J5 ✉ Georgenstrasse
☎ 2082645 🕐 Wed–Mon 11–6 🚇 U- or S-Bahn Friedrichstrasse

BERGMANNSTRASSE
Scents and flavours of the Orient will assail your senses in this Kreuzberg street from the fruit, vegetables, spices and kebab stalls.

➕ J8 ✉ Bergmannstrasse
🚇 U-Bahn Gneisenaustrasse

BERLINER KUNST-UND-NOSTALGIE-MARKT
Art and nostalgia – for the most part paintings, drawings and antiques.

➕ J5 ✉ Am Kupfergraben
🕐 Sat–Sun 11–5 🚇 U- or S-Bahn Friedrichstrasse

CONFISERIE MELANIE
Quirky but delightful, this established store specialises in confections that may surprise, even shock, your taste buds.

➕ C6 ✉ Goethestrasse 4
☎ 3138330 🕐 Mon–Fri 10–7; Sat 10–2 🚇 U-Bahn Bismarckstrasse

ENOTECA
Proprietor Werner Blanck is a great connoisseur of Italian wines.

➕ E7 ✉ Ludwig-Kirch-Strasse 11 ☎ 88679960 🚇 U-Bahn Uhlandstrasse

FLOHMARKT
Genuine bargains at knockdown prices in the Tacheles building.

➕ J4 ✉ Oranienburger Strasse
🕐 Sat–Sun 8AM–3PM
🚇 S-Bahn Oranienburger Strasse

KADEWE FOOD HALL
Europe's largest delicatessen. Food and drink from around the world: lobster and caviar, exotic vegetables and spices – and over 1,000 varieties of German sausage.

✉ Sixth floor, KaDeWe (➤ 70)

KING'S TEAGARTEN
More than 200 varieties of tea from all over the world, and classical music to enjoy as well.

➕ D7 ✉ Ku'damm 217
☎ 8837059 🕐 Daily 9–7
🚇 U-Bahn Uhlandstrasse

TRÖDEL MARKT
A market in the Tiergarten popular with antiques dealers and tourists.

➕ E5 ✉ Strasse des 17 Juni
☎ 3228199 🕐 Weekends
🚇 S-Bahn Tiergarten

TURKISH MARKET
An intriguing market in the heart of the Turkish community, offering choice ethnic food including olives, cheeses and spiced chicken.

➕ L8 ✉ Maybachufer
☎ 68092926 🕐 Tue–Fri noon–6:30 🚇 U-Bahn Schönleinstrasse

WINTERFELDTMARKT
A favourite with Berliners, this Schöneberg market is one of the city's liveliest. Have brunch in one of the local cafés.

➕ F7 ✉ Winterfeldtplatz
🕐 Wed and Sat 8–1
🚇 U-Bahn Nollendorfplatz

WINTERFELDTPLATZ

One pleasant way to while away a Saturday morning is to explore the antiques shops around Motzstrasse, before homing in on one of Berlin's most colourful and entertaining street markets, in Winterfeldtplatz. You never know quite what you will find here, which is the main attraction – everything from hand-me-down jewellery to books with faded covers, from flowers to children's clothes. Having worked up an appetite, visit one of the numerous cafés serving breakfast in the vicinity – try Tim's Canadian Deli on Maassenstrasse (➤ 69).

The Best of the Rest

FRIEDRICHSTRASSE

Rebuilt almost from scratch during the last decade, Friedrichstrasse is rapidly becoming a magnet for discerning shoppers, especially aficionados of the latest designer fashions. Galeries Lafayette (➤ 70), also here, is the first branch of the famous department store outside France. Apart from Jean Nouvel's highly innovative open-plan design, the main talking point is the mouth-watering Food Hall, selling everything from pâtés to oysters.

BERLINER ZINNFIGUREN

A magical collection of handmade tin soldiers; also dancing couples, circus animals and other delightful figurines.
➕ D7 ✉ Knesebeckstrasse 88 ☎ 3157000 🚊 S-Bahn Savignyplatz

DER RIOJA WEINSPEZIALIST

The 'Rioja Specialist' stocks all varieties of wines originating in the Iberian Peninsula.
➕ Off map ✉ Steglitzer Damm 29 ☎ 7966190 🚊 S-Bahn Südende

DER TEELADEN

Berlin's largest tea emporium.
➕ D7 ✉ Kurfürstendamm 209 ☎ 8819181 🚊 U-Bahn Uhlandstrasse

DUSSMANN

This huge book and record store is ideal for last-minute present buying – you could even do all your shopping here. Where CDs are concerned, if they don't have it here, you won't find it anywhere.
➕ J5 ✉ Friedrichstrasse 90 ☎ 20252059 🕐 Mon–Sat 10AM–10PM 🚊 U-Bahn Friedrichstrasse

EUROPA-CENTER

Not only an entertainment complex, the Europa-Center is also Berlin's largest and best-known indoor shopping centre. There are more than 100 shops in all, on three floors, plus many bars and coffee shops.
➕ E6 ✉ Tauentzienstrasse 🚊 U-Bahn Kurfürstendamm

HAUS AM CHECKPOINT CHARLIE

The only place in Berlin where you can still find an authentic piece of the Wall; also GDR and Soviet Union medals, military insignia and much more.
➕ J6 ✉ Friedrichstrasse 44 ☎ 2537250 🚊 U-Bahn Kochstrasse

J UND M FÄSSLER

Wide selection of toys, souvenirs and curiosities.
➕ E6 ✉ Europa-Center, Tauentzienstrasse ☎ 2614807 🚊 U-Bahn Kurfürstendamm

KIEPERT

The city's largest collection of books about Berlin.
➕ E6 ✉ Hardenbergstrasse 4–5 ☎ 311880 🚊 U-Bahn Zoologischer Garten
Also at:
➕ J5 ✉ Friedrichstrasse 63 🚊 U- or S-Bahn Friedrichstrasse

KONSTANZA

Organic vegetables, fruit, wine, and even cosmetics, are the stock in trade of this Wilmersdorf emporium.
➕ D7 ✉ Konstanzer Strasse 10 ☎ 8813428 🚊 U-Bahn Konstanzer Strasse

KULTURKAUFHAUS

This enormous bookstore in the heart of the Mitte has huge stocks of videos, CDs and computer software. There is also a 'cookie café' offering a good selection of cookies based on original American recipes.
➕ J5 ✉ Friedrichstrasse 90 ☎ 20251111 🚊 U- or S-Bahn Friedrichstrasse

KUNSTBUCHHAND-LUNG GALERIE 2000

Art books from all over the world.

⊞ D5 ✉ Knesebeckstrasse 56–8 ☎ 8838467 Ⓠ U-Bahn Uhlandstrasse

MAISON DE LA DANSE

Purveyors of all kinds of dancewear, from tutus to tango dresses.

⊞ D6 ✉ Pestalozzistrasse 60 ☎ 3232043 Ⓠ S-Bahn Savignyplatz

MARGA SCHOELLER

The best selection of fiction and non-fiction books in English in Berlin.

⊞ D7 ✉ Knesebeckstrasse 33–4 ☎ 8811112 Ⓠ S-Bahn Savignyplatz

MUSIKANTIQUARIAT ROBERT HARTWIG

Musical, theatrical and film ephemera.

⊞ D6 ✉ Pestalozzistrasse 23 ☎ 3129124 Ⓠ S-Bahn Savignyplatz

MUSIKHAUS RIEDL

Classical music – CDs, tapes and cheap music.

⊞ J5 ✉ Koncerthaus am Gendarmenmarkt ☎ 8827395 Ⓠ U-Bahn Stadtmitte

PARFUM NACH GEWICHT 'PERFUME BY WEIGHT'

Lehmann's is a perfumery with a difference. All the scents are home-made. The staff will fill a bottle with the fragrance of your choice – or you can mix your own.

⊞ D6 ✉ Kantstrasse 106 ☎ 3243582 Ⓠ U-Bahn Wilmersdorfer Strasse

POSTERGALERIE 200

The emphasis here is on the quirky and offbeat.

⊞ E7 ✉ Ku'damm 195 ☎ 8821959 Ⓠ U-Bahn Kurfürstendamm

SKI HÜTTE

If you have the sudden urge to play tennis or to go sailing on the Havel, you can be fitted out here. Every type of sports equipment.

⊞ E6 ✉ Joachimstalerstrasse 42 ☎ 8811480 Ⓠ U- or S-Bahn Zoologischer Garten

SPIELEN BERLIN

Toys of the traditional handmade variety.

⊞ K4 ✉ Neue Schönhauser Strasse 8 ☎ 2817183 Ⓒ Mon–Fri 9:30AM–7PM; Sat 9:30AM–3PM Ⓠ U-Bahn Hackescher Markt

STROH-KUNSTHANDWERK

Handmade toys and traditional crafts near the Hackescher Höfe.

⊞ K4 ✉ Sophienstrasse 9 ☎ 2826754 Ⓠ S-Bahn Hackescher Markt

THE BRITISH BOOKSHOP

Wide selection of English-language books.

⊞ J5 ✉ Mauerstrasse 83–4 ☎ 2384680 Ⓠ U-Bahn Mohrenstrasse

WIEDENHOFF

Solingen cutlery, replica swords, helmets, armour and decorative weapons are available here.

⊞ E6 ✉ Europa-Center, Tauentzienstrasse ☎ 2612730 Ⓠ U-Bahn Kufürstendamm

EUROPA-CENTER

There are more than 100 shops in the high-rise shopping mall known as the Europa-Center. The Mercedes star on the roof is something of a landmark and when you have finished your shopping you can take the lift to the viewing platform on the 22nd floor for unbeatable views of Berlin. There is a tourist information office here, too, and you may find yourself returning in the evening for a visit to the cinema, cabaret, or to go to a disco.

Theatres & Concerts

DEUTSCHE STAATSOPER

The handsome neoclassical building dominating Bebelplatz is Berlin's oldest opera house, the Deutsche Staatsoper, built in the reign of Frederick the Great. It is currently engaged in a life-and-death struggle with its chief rival, the Deutsche Oper, for fast-diminishing government subsidies. The roll-call of musicians who have graced this stage is amazing – it includes the composers Mendelssohn, Meyerbeer, Liszt and Richard Strauss, the legendary conductor Wilhelm Furtwängler and, more recently, the pianist Daniel Barenboim.

BERLINER ENSEMBLE

Playwright Bertolt Brecht founded this famous theatre company in 1948, and his plays are still in the repertoire.
✚ J4 ✉ Bertolt-Brecht-Platz ☎ 28408155 🚇 U- or S-Bahn Friedrichstrasse

DEUTSCHE OPER BERLIN

Opera and modern ballet in an uninspired post-war concert hall.
✚ C6 ✉ Bismarckstrasse 35 ☎ 3410249 🚇 U-Bahn Deutsche Oper

DEUTSCHE STAATSOPER

Opera and ballet in a beautiful baroque concert hall, now restored after extensive wartime bomb damage.
✚ J5 ✉ Unter den Linden 7 ☎ 20354555 🚇 U-Bahn Französische Strasse

DEUTSCHES THEATER

The name of theatre director Max Reinhardt was virtually synonymous with the life of this theatre from the turn of the century until the Nazis came to power. Film stars Pola Negri and Marlene Dietrich performed here.
✚ H4 ✉ Schumannstrasse 13 ☎ 28441225 🚇 U-Bahn Oranienburger Tor

METROPOL-THEATER

Musicals, shows and operettas strong in the heart of the Mitte.
✚ J5 ✉ Friedrichstrasse 101 ☎ 20364117 🚇 U- or S-Bahn Friedrichstrasse

MUSICAL THEATER BERLIN

Berlin's newest venue for productions of musicals, such as Disney's *Hunchback of Notre Dame*.
✚ H6 ✉ Potsdamer Platz ☎ 018054444 🚇 U- or S-Bahn Potsdamer Platz

PHILHARMONIE

One of the world's most famous orchestras, the Berlin Philharmonic, performs in Hans Scharoun's 1960s architectural masterpiece in the Kulturforum. The acoustics are impeccable, tickets are rare as gold dust.
✚ G6 ✉ Herbert-von-Karajan-Strasse ☎ 254880 🚇 U- or S-Bahn Potsdamer Platz

SCHAUSPIELHAUS BERLIN (KONZERTHAUS)

The magnificent concert hall of the Berlin Symphony Orchestra was designed by architect Karl Friedrich Schinkel in 1818.
✚ J5 ✉ Gendarmenmarkt 2 ☎ 203092100 🚇 U-Bahn Französische Strasse

THEATER DES WESTENS

Broadway shows.
✚ E6 ✉ Kantstrasse 12 ☎ 8822888 🚇 U- or S-Bahn Zoologischer Garten

UFA-FABRIK

A well-known spot for alternative music, dance, film and theatre in Kreuzberg. Popular with young Berliners.
✚ Off map to south ✉ Viktoriastrasse 13 ☎ 755030 🚇 U-Bahn Ullsteinstrasse

Cabaret

BAR JEDER VERNUNFT

Eat, drink and enjoy the show – there's also a piano bar.

✚ E7 ✉ Schaperstrasse 24 ☎ 8831582 Ⓜ U-Bahn Augsburger Strasse

CHAMÄLEON VARIETÉ

Variety at its most expansive in an art-deco setting. Clowns, acrobats, magicians and more; much loved by Berliners.

✚ K4 ✉ Rosenthaler Strasse 40–1 ☎ 2827118 Ⓜ S-Bahn Hackescher Markt

CHEZ NOUS

Famous for its transvestite shows, and still going strong after more than 30 years. Book ahead.

✚ E7 ✉ Marburger Strasse 14 ☎ 2131810 Ⓜ U-Bahn Kurfürstendamm

DIE DISTEL

'The Thistle' club is known for its acerbic political satire.

✚ J5 ✉ Friedrichstrasse 101 ☎ 2044704 Ⓜ U- or S-Bahn Friedrichstrasse

FRIEDRICHSTADT-PALAST

The most famous nightspot in eastern Berlin, with a long tradition. In the main revue entertainment includes variety acts, a floor show and loud music; the small revue is more intimate.

✚ J5 ✉ Friedrichstrasse 107 ☎ 232620 Ⓜ U- or S-Bahn Friedrichstrasse

LA VIE EN ROSE

Glamorous showgirls in feathers and pearls sing their hearts out.

✚ J9 ✉ Tempelhof Airport ☎ 69513000 Ⓜ Tue–Sun from 9PM Ⓜ U-Bahn Platz der Luftbrücke

KABARETT DIE STACHELSCHWEINE

The political satire here is tame and barely merits the prickly associations in the name (Stachelschwein means porcupine).

✚ E6 ✉ Europa-Center ☎ 2614795 Ⓜ U-Bahn Kurfürstendamm

KABARETT DIE WÜHLMÄUSE

'The Voles' offers some of the best and sharpest political satire in Berlin.

✚ E7 ✉ Nürnburger Strasse 33 ☎ 2137047 Ⓜ U-Bahn Augsburger Strasse

MEHRINGHOF THEATER

A Kreuzberg theatre specialising in radical or alternative cabaret.

✚ J8 ✉ Gneisenaustrasse 2a ☎ 6915099 Ⓜ U-Bahn Gneisenaustrasse

WINTERGARTEN VARIETE

Long synonymous with late-night entertainment, the Wintergarten makes for a fun-packed evening. International variety entertainers star.

✚ G7 ✉ Potsdamerstrasse 96 ☎ 23088230 Ⓜ U-Bahn Kurfürstenstrasse

GOODBYE TO CABARET?

The 1920s was the undisputed golden age of cabaret, a fact seized upon by Bob Fosse in his 1972 film musical Cabaret, based on Christopher Isherwood's novel Goodbye to Berlin. The main characteristics of the art form – biting political satire and unabashed sexual licence – aroused the wrath of the Nazi ideologues, who closed down the theatres and arrested many of the performers. Since World War II, Berliners have done their best to revive the tradition but the modern clubs are often more like variety shows – the bite is missing.

LANGUAGE PROBLEMS?

Even if you don't speak German, you will probably still enjoy the song and dance element of cabaret shows. However, in order to understand the political satire, some knowledge of the German language and a familiarity with current affairs is needed.

Pubs, Bars & Clubs

LOCAL TIPPLES

A favourite local drink is *Berliner Weisse*, beer with a dash of raspberry or woodruff syrup (*mit Grün*) – addictive if you have a sweet tooth. This is a traditional beverage; more trendy is *Herva mit Mosel*, a peculiar blend of white wine with maté tea that Berliners now consume at least half a million times annually. Hardened drinkers prefer *Korn*, frothy beer with a schnapps chaser.

BAR AM LÜTZOWPLATZ
Cocktail bar with one of the longest happy hours in Berlin (5PM–9PM) and a clientele that likes to see and be seen.
F6 ✉ Lützowplatz 7 ☎ 2626807 ⏰ Daily from 3PM 🚇 U-Bahn Nollendorfplatz

BIG EDEN
Once famous for the international celebrities who used to drop in, Big Eden is now a conventional dance club attracting mainly local teenagers and visitors.
D7 ✉ Ku'damm 202 ☎ 8826120 ⏰ Nightly from 8PM 🚇 U-Bahn Kurfürstendamm

CAFÉ SILBERSTEIN
One of a crop of trendy new bars in the Mitte. Here you can snack on sushi if you can make your order heard above the music.
J4 ✉ Oranienburgerstrasse 27 ☎ 2812095 ⏰ Daily 4PM–4AM 🚇 U-Bahn Oranienburger Tor

DOLMEN
Lively nightspot featuring DJs and live bands.
K4 ✉ Schönhauser Allee 6–7 ☎ 4406030 ⏰ Thu–Sat 11PM–5AM 🚇 U-Bahn Rosa Luxemburg Platz

EL BARRIO
Popular cellar bar with salsa music. Occasional live bands and salsa classes.
G7 ✉ Potsdamer Strasse 84 ☎ 2621852 ⏰ Daily from 10PM 🚇 U-Bahn Kurfürstenstrasse

FAR OUT
A conventional nightclub for the younger crowd, in Berlin's west end. The music tends to be mainstream rock and pop.
D7 ✉ Ku'damm 156 ☎ 32000717 ⏰ Tue–Sun 10PM–late 🚇 U-Bahn Adenauerplatz

FOGO
This Kreuzberg cocktail bar draws an interesting, mainly young crowd.
J8 ✉ Arndtstrasse 29 ☎ 6921465 ⏰ Daily 8:30PM–6AM 🚇 U-Bahn Gneisenaustrasse

GAINSBOURG
Named after the famous 1960s French singer, this nightclub plays a raunchy selection of French music.
D6 ✉ Savignyplatz 5 ☎ 3137464 ⏰ Daily 5PM–3AM 🚇 S-Bahn Savignyplatz

HARRY'S NEW YORK BAR
This piano bar in the Hotel Esplanade attracts a mainly business clientele and is suitably restrained.
G6 ✉ Lützowufer 15 ☎ 254780/261011 ⏰ Daily noon–3AM 🚇 U-Bahn Kurfürstenstrasse

KUMPELNEST 3000
This former brothel, a dance mecca since the 1980s, attracts party-goers of all ages and persuasions. Expect a crowd at weekends.
G6 ✉ Lützow Strasse 23 ☎ 2616918 ⏰ Daily from 5PM 🚇 U-Bahn Nollendorfplatz

LEYDICKE

One of the oldest pubs in Berlin, dating from 1877, and among the most atmospheric. The bar pours a celebrated selection of liqueurs and unusual wines flavoured with cherry, gooseberry and the like.

🚇 G8 ✉ Mansteinstrasse 4
☎ 2162973 🕐 Mon, Tue, Thu, Fri 4PM–midnight; Wed, Sat, Sun 11AM–1AM 🚇 U- or S-Bahn Yorckstrasse

90 GRAD

This popular club can get very crowded in the wee hours. The music veers between hip-hop and techno, with a little soul for good measure.

🚇 G7 ✉ Dennewitzstrasse 37
☎ 2628984 🕐 Wed–Sun from 11PM 🚇 U-Bahn Kurfürstenstrasse

OXYMORON

Busy café-restaurant in one of the courtyards of Hackesche Höfe with a dance club to the rear. The music is eclectic: soft rock, drum'n'bass, hip-hop and such.

🚇 K4 ✉ Rosenthaler Strasse 40–1 ☎ 28391886 🕐 Daily 10PM–4AM 🚇 S-Bahn Hackescher Markt

QUINNS

An Irish pub and restaurant in Prenzlauer Berg where the cocktails are half-price between 5PM and 7:30PM.

🚇 K4 ✉ Schönhauser Allee 6–7 ☎ 4406030
🕐 Mon–Thu 11AM–1AM; Fri–Sat noon–3AM; Sun noon–1AM
🚇 U-Bahn Rosa Luxemburg Platz

ROTE HARFE

One of a crop of lively modern cafés in Kreuzberg, the Red Harp is warm, welcoming and a touch sophisticated.

🚇 L7 ✉ Oranienstrasse 13
☎ 6184446 🕐 Daily 8AM–late 🚇 U-Bahn Kottbusser Tor

SLUMBERLAND

Late-night stopover for footsore party-goers.

🚇 F7 ✉ Goltzstrasse 24
☎ 2165349 🕐 10PM–late 🚇 U-Bahn Nollendorfplatz

TRESOR 30

An old favourite that has stood the test of time. Berlin techno was born here.

🚇 H6 ✉ Leipziger Strasse 126a ☎ No phone
🕐 Wed–Sun from 11PM
🚇 U- or S-Bahn Potsdamer Platz

ZUM ELEFANTEN

This bar is a popular Kreuzberg meeting place.

🚇 L7 ✉ Oranienstrasse 12
☎ 6123013 🕐 Daily 11AM–1AM 🚇 U-Bahn Kottbusser Tor

ZUR LETZTEN INSTANZ

Dating from 1621, the oldest pub in Berlin serves traditional fare. The name translates as 'at the last resort', recalling the time when this was a stopping-off point for condemned criminals. The menu is full of judicial references.

🚇 L5 ✉ Waisenstrasse 14–16
☎ 2425528 🕐 Daily noon–1AM 🚇 U-Bahn Klosterstrasse

MUSIC FOR ALL

Musical tastes have splintered remarkably in recent years; in Berlin this is reflected by the plethora of specialist nightclubs. Bebop, house, soul, jungle, ragga, techno and heavy metal – pay your money and take your choice.

Folk, Jazz & Rock

JAZZ FESTIVAL

The annual Berlin Jazz Festival takes place at the beginning of November and lasts just 3 or 4 days. The main venue is the Haus der Kulturen der Welt in the Tiergarten. Advance information is available from:

Berliner Festspielie
✉ Budapester Strasse 50
☎ 254890
To book ahead, consult:
Fullhouse Service
✉ Budapester Strasse 50
☎ 25489254

ARENA

An old bus depot in the Treptow district, now a major venue for headline rock and pop bands.
✚ H8 ✉ Eichenstrasse 4
☎ 5337333 Ⓢ U-Bahn Schlesisches Tor

A-TRANE JAZZCLUB

This Charlottenburg night haunt caters to lovers of modern jazz and bebop. Concerts usually start at about 10PM.
✚ D7 ✉ Bleibtreustrasse 1
☎ 3132550 Ⓢ S-Bahn Savignyplatz

B FLAT

Occasional live jazz performances. There isn't usually an entrance fee.
✚ K4 ✉ Rosenthaler Strasse 13 ☎ 2806349 Ⓢ S-Bahn Hackescher Markt

EISSPORTHALLE

This ice hockey stadium sometimes doubles as a rock and pop hall; in summer, concerts are also held in the summer garden of the Messegelände complex next door.
✚ A7 ✉ Jafféstrasse
☎ 30380 Ⓢ S-Bahn Westkreuz

HAUS DER KULTUREN DER WELT

Berliners now call the formerly named Kongresshalle, in the Tiergarten, the 'pregnant oyster' because of the distinctive shape of its curved roof. It regularly hosts rock music fans.
✚ G5 ✉ John-Foster-Dulles-Allee ☎ 39700513 Ⓢ S-Bahn Unter den Linden

ICC BERLIN (INTERNATIONAL CONGRESS CENTRE)

There are two rock and pop halls in this enormous conference centre.
✚ B6 ✉ Messedamm 22
☎ 30380 Ⓢ S-Bahn Witzleben

QUASIMODO

Stifling and crowded, this is as good a place as any to hear live jazz, blues and funk. Tickets are available from 3PM on the day of performance.
✚ E6 ✉ Kantstrasse 12a
☎ 3128086 Ⓢ U- or S-Bahn Zoologischer Garten

SOPHIENCLUB

A venue with a history going back to the days of the Communists. The music could be anything from jazz or soul to funk, house or reggae, depending on which night you're here.
✚ K4 ✉ Sophienstrasse 6
☎ 2824552 Ⓢ U-Bahn Weinmeisterstrasse

TRÄNENPALAST

The 'Palace of Tears' is anything but. Rock and pop concerts, discos and cabaret all happen here.
✚ J5 ✉ Reichstagufer 17
☎ 20610011 Ⓢ U- or S-Bahn Friedrichstrasse

WALDBÜHNE

Berlin's most famous rock venue, this open-air arena, seating 20,000, regularly hosts some of the world's most prestigious bands.
✚ Off map to west
✉ Glockenturmstrasse/Passenheimer Strasse 1–19
☎ 23088230 Ⓢ S-Bahn Pickelsberg

Sport

ARTS VITALIS

Modern fitness centre with aerobics, weights, sauna and pool. Open to non-members.

🔲 F9 ✉ Hauptstrasse 19
☎ 7883563 🚇 U-Bahn Rathaus Schöneberg

BLUB

Berlin's most famous swimming pool, with indoor and outdoor facilities, boasts Europe's longest 'superslide' (120m). Sauna and children's play area.

➕ Off map to south
✉ Buschkrugallee 64
☎ 6066060 🍴 Restaurant and café 🚇 U-Bahn Grenzallee

FEZ (FREIZEIT-UND-ERHOLUNGSZENTRUM WUHLHEIDE)

A leisure centre in pleasant Köpenick with a swimming pool.

➕ Off map to southeast
✉ An der Wuhlheide
☎ 53071504 🍴 Café
🚇 S-Bahn Wuhlheide

OLYMPIASTADION

This stadium was built to host the 1936 Olympics. Football matches take place here, and the pool is open to the public.

➕ Off map to west
✉ Olympische Platz
☎ 300633 🍴 Café
🚇 U-Bahn Olympiastadion (Ost)

SEEBAD FRIEDRICHSHAGEN

A beach on the eastern side of the city offering a less crowded alternative to Wannsee in the west.

➕ Off map to southeast
✉ Müggelseedamm 216
☎ 6487777 🍴 Café
🚇 S-Bahn Friedrichshagen

SPORT UND ERHOLUNGSZENTRUM

The SEZ has a fitness studio, swimming pool, volleyball courts, bowling alley and skating rinks.

🔲 N4 ✉ Landsberger Allee 77
☎ 421820 🍴 Café
🚇 S-Bahn Landsberger Allee

SPORTPARK KARLSHORST

Enormous multi-sport fitness centre equipped with the latest fitness machinery. Squash, tennis and badminton courts, saunas, solarium and restaurant.

➕ Off map to southeast
✉ Zwieseler Strasse 50
☎ 5099391 🍴 Restaurant
🚇 S-Bahn Karlshorst

STRANDBAD WANNSEE

Wannsee's open-air pool and facilities date from the 1930s but have worn well. Near large beach.

➕ Off map to southwest
✉ Wannseebadweg
☎ 8035450 🍴 Café
🚇 S-Bahn Wannsee

TENNIS AND SQUASH CITY

The Wilmersdorf complex has 18 squash and tennis courts.

➕ Off map to south
✉ Brandenburgische Strasse 53
☎ 8739097 🚇 U-Bahn Konstanzer-Strasse

TRABRENNBAHN MARIENDORF

Trotting races usually take place on Sundays at this suburban racetrack.

➕ Off map to south
✉ Mariendorfer Damm 222–98
☎ 74104250 🚇 U-Bahn Alt Mariendorf

CYCLING

Cycling is increasingly popular with Berliners. But beware – cyclists pay scant regard to pedestrians. Bike lights at night, though legally required, seem to be a luxury that many can do without. So, if you hear the frantic ringing of a bell – watch out.

Luxury Hotels

HOTEL PRICES

Expect to pay the following prices per night for a double room, but it's always worth asking when you make your reservation whether any special deals are available.

Luxury	over 153 euros; DM300
Mid-range	up to 153 euros: DM300
Budget	up to 76.5 euros; DM150

HOTEL LOCATIONS

You can stay virtually anywhere in Berlin, but hotels tend to cluster around the Ku'damm. Charlottenburg and Schöneberg are quieter yet equally convenient. The establishments spawned by the East German authorities, such as the Forum on Alexanderplatz, are trying desperately to cope with the chill winds of economic competition. The most scenic locations are Tegel, Wannsee, the Grunewald forest and Müggelsee.

ADLON HOTEL

This historic 337-room hotel, at the Brandenburg Gate is one of the city's most luxurious.

✚ H5 ✉ Unter den Linden 77 ☎ 22610; Fax 22612222 🔊 S-Bahn Unter den Linden

ALSTERHOF

This 1960s hotel, located near the Europa-Center, has 200 rooms, a pool and a fitness centre.

✚ C7 ✉ Augsburger Strasse 5 ☎ 212420; Fax 2183949 🔊 U-Bahn Augsburger Strasse

BERLIN EXCELSIOR HOTEL

Duplex suites, garden terrace, 317 rooms and several restaurants and bars. Near Zoo Station.

✚ E6 ✉ Hardenbergstrasse 14 ☎ 31550; Fax 31551002 🔊 U- or S-Bahn Zoologischer Garten

BERLIN HILTON

500 rooms, plus bars, restaurants, fitness centre, pool and fabulous views over the Gendarmenmarkt.

✚ J6 ✉ Mohrenstrasse 30 ☎ 20230; Fax 20234269 🔊 U-Bahn Stadtmitte

BRISTOL HOTEL KEMPINSKI

Almost all of Berlin's traditional hotels were destroyed during World War II, but some names live on. This hotel trades on an established reputation for courteous and attentive service. Chandeliers and deep carpets recall its resplendent past. 315 rooms, 44 suites, fitness room and swimming pool.

✚ B7 ✉ Ku'damm 27

☎ 884340; Fax 8836075 🔊 U-Bahn Adenauerplatz

GRAND HYATT

One of Berlin's newest hotels, the Grand Hyatt has 340 rooms, and a swimming pool and fitness centre with city views.

✚ H6 ✉ Marlene-Dietrich-Platz 2 ☎ 25531234; Fax 25531235 🔊 U- or S-Bahn Potsdamer Platz

INTER-CONTINENTAL BERLIN

Berlin's most glamorous hotel has 510 rooms, 70 suites, a swimming pool, sauna and business centre.

✚ F6 ✉ Budapester Strasse 2 ☎ 26020; Fax 26022600 🔊 U- or S-Bahn Zoologischer Garten

RESIDENZ BERLIN

Jugendstil architecture is one of the boasts of this 80-room hotel near the Ku'damm. Good restaurant.

✚ E7 ✉ Meinekestrasse 9 ☎ 884430; Fax 8824726 🔊 U-Bahn Kurfürstendamm

SAVOY HOTEL

An elegant hotel with large roof terrace and 125 rooms. A few minutes walk from the Ku'damm.

✚ E7 ✉ Fasanenstrasse 9–10 ☎ 311030; Fax 31103333 🔊 U-Bahn Uhlandstrasse

THE WESTIN GRAND

A five-storey, ultra-modern hotel with 358 rooms, swimming pool and sauna. In Friedrichstrasse.

✚ J5 ✉ Friedrichstrasse 158–164 ☎ 20270; Fax 20273362 🔊 U- or S-Bahn Friedrichstrasse

Mid-Range Hotels

BERLIN PLAZA HOTEL

This hotel, near the Ku'damm, has 131 rooms and a restaurant with a terrace.

✚ D7 ✉ Knesebeckstrasse 63
☎ 884130; Fax 88413754
🚇 U-Bahn Uhlandstrasse

FJORD HOTEL

Clean and modern, this 55-room hotel is convenient for the Kulturforum. Roof terrace open for breakfast in summer.

✚ G7 ✉ Bissingzeile 13
☎ 254720; Fax 25472111
🚇 U-Bahn Kurfürstenstrasse

HOTEL ASTORIA

This 32-room hotel is situated among the art galleries of Fasanenstrasse. Bar and baby-sitting service.

✚ E6 ✉ Fasanenstrasse 2
☎ 3124067; Fax 3125027
🚇 U-Bahn Uhlandstrasse

HOTEL BRANDENBURGER HOF

A stylish building dating back to the Wilhelmine era of the late 19th to early 20th century. Not far from the Kaiser Wilhelm Memorial Church. Winter garden restaurant and 82 rooms.

✚ E7 ✉ Eislebener Strasse 14
☎ 214050; Fax 21405100
🚇 U-Bahn Augsburger Strasse

HOTEL JURINE

Friendly, family-run hotel close to Prenzlauer Berg. All 50 bright and airy rooms have pay and satellite TV.

✚ K3 ✉ Schwedter Strasse 15
☎ 4432990; Fax 44329999
🚇 U-Bahn Senefelderplatz

HOTEL KRONPRINZ BERLIN

An elegant, 66-room hotel at the end of the Ku'damm.

✚ B7 ✉ Kronprinzendamm 1
☎ 896030; Fax 8931215
🚇 S-Bahn Halensee

HOTEL RIEHMERS HOFGARTEN

This florid stucco apartment house was built in 1891 for prosperous Berliners. Now refurbished it has 20 decent-sized rooms.

✚ J8 ✉ Yorckstrasse 83
☎ 78098800; Fax 78098808
🚇 U-Bahn Mehringdamm

HOTEL UNTER DEN LINDEN

A modern hotel on the corner of Friedrichstrasse and Unter den Linden, with 331 rooms and suites, restaurant, bar and conference facilities.

✚ J5 ✉ Unter den Linden 14
☎ 238110; Fax 23811100
🚇 U- or S-Bahn Friedrichstrasse

HOTEL VILLA KASTANIA

Comfortable hotel in Charlottenburg. The 43 rooms have good facilities, and there is a pool.

✚ A6 ✉ Kastanienallee 20
☎ 3000020; Fax 30000210
🚇 U-Bahn Theodor-Heuss-Platz

LA VIE HOTEL JOACHIMSHOF

Comfortable and modern 35-room hotel, opposite the Natural History Museum. A metro stop away from the Mitte. Small bar, restaurant and sauna.

✚ H4 ✉ Invalidenstrassse 98
☎ 203956100; Fax 203956199
🚇 U-Bahn Zinnowitzer Strasse

HOTEL HEINEKE ARTE

The 60 high-ceilinged rooms of this comfortable hotel are decorated in an old-fashioned bourgeois style, with a modern art touch. A carpeted staircase leads to the first-floor reception desk and the breakfast room is hung with contemporary art. Although this mid-priced hotel is located in the side street of Heinekestrasse, just 200 metres from the Ku'damm, it's quiet.

☎ 88678190; Fax 88679292

Budget Accommodation

WHERE TO LOOK

Berlin offers a surprising variety of lower-priced accommodation and you do not necessarily need to trek out to the backwoods. Schöneberg and Kreuzberg districts both have a plentiful supply of pensions and simple hotels, most of which are clean and up to scratch. Young people may prefer Kreuzberg for its lively night scene.

YOUTH HOSTELS

Youth hostels (jugendgästehaus or jugendherberge) do not impose restrictions on age or families but to stay in them you do need to be a member of the Youth Hostel Association (YHA). You can buy a membership card from your own national YHA, on arrival at the youth hostel, or from the:

Mitgliederservice des DJH Berlin-Brandenburg
✉ Tempelhofer Ufer 32
☎ 2649520; Fax 2640437
You can obtain either a fully valid membership or a guest card with a welcome stamp for each night of your stay. Family membership is also available.

A & O

Inexpensive rooms in the old east end. Multilingual staff, 30 beds, cut-price meals and bike hire.
✚ Off map to east
✉ Boxhagener Strasse 73
☎ 29007365 🚆 S-Bahn Ostkreuz

AM KROSSINSEE

Köpenick campsite run by the German Camping Club (DCC). Open year round.
✚ Off map to southeast
✉ Wernsdorfer Strasse 45
☎ 6758687; Fax 6759150
🚆 S-Bahn Köpenick

CIRCUS

City centre hostel for backpackers. Luggage store, bike hire, ticket service and 24-hour reception.
✚ J4 ✉ Rosa-Luxemburg-Strasse 39–41 ☎ 28391433; Fax 28391484 🚇 U-Bahn Rosa-Luxemburg-Platz

DIE FABRIK

Friendly hostel in an old brick factory building, convenient for Kreuzberg.
✚ M7 ✉ Schlesische Strasse 18 ☎ 6117116; Fax 6182974 🚇 U-Bahn Schlesisches Tor

FRAUEN HOTEL ARTEMISIA

Just for women – with eight attractive rooms, a bar and a library. In Wilmersdorf. Book early.
✚ C7 ✉ Brandenburgische Strasse 18 ☎ 8738905; Fax 8628653 🚇 U-Bahn Adenauerplatz

HOTEL TRANSIT

One of the best hotels in the lower price range – with 49 clean rooms and surprisingly good facilities.
✚ J8 ✉ Hagelberger Strasse 53–4 ☎ 7890470; Fax 78904777 🚇 U-Bahn Mehringdamm

JUGENDGÄSTEHAUS AM WANNSEE

A clean and friendly youth hostel, with 264 beds, in the scenic Grunewald.
✚ Off map to west
✉ Badeweg 1 ☎ 8032035; Fax 8035908 🚆 S-Bahn Nikolassee

JUGENDHERBERGE BERLIN INTERNATIONAL

Popular youth hostel with 358 beds. Book ahead.
✚ G6 ✉ Kluckstrasse 3 ☎ 2611098; Fax 2650383 🚇 U-Bahn Kurfürstenstrasse

JUGENDHERBERGE ERNST REUTER

Comfortable hostel with 111 beds, luggage store and a garden.
✚ Off map to northwest
✉ Hermsdorfer Damm 48-50 ☎ 4041610; Fax 4045972 🚇 U-Bahn Alt-Tegel

MITTE'S BACKPACKER

This 20-bed hostel caters to backpackers. Information service and bike hire.
✚ H3 ✉ Chausseestrasse 102 ☎ 28390965; Fax 28390935 🚇 U-Bahn Zinnowitzerstrasse

PENSION KREUZBERG

A favourite with youngsters and backpackers. Near Kreuzberg.
✚ J7 ✉ Grossebeerenstrasse 64 ☎ 2511362 🚇 U-Bahn Mehringdamm

BERLIN
travel facts

Arriving & Departing *88*

Essential Facts *89–90*

Public Transport *90–91*

Media & Communications *91–92*

Emergencies *92–93*

Language *93*

ARRIVING & DEPARTING

Before you go

- EU nationals need a valid passport or a national identity card. Citizens of the US, Canada, Australia and New Zealand need a valid passport to stay for up to three months. Other nationals should check visa requirements with the German Embassy.
- No compulsory vaccinations are needed, but make sure you have up-to-date tetanus and polio immunisation.
- Obtain a form E111 from the post office to cover any emergency medical treatment.

When to go

- Expect some rain at any time, and some unusually hot and humid weather in summer.
- April to June is the most comfortable period.
- The arts scene is liveliest between October and May.

Climate

- Average temperatures are -1°C (29°F) in January, 10°C (50°F) in April, 20°C (68°F) in July and 10°C (50°F) in October.

Arriving by air

- All major carriers fly to Berlin.
- Berlin has three international airports (Tegel, Schönefeld and Tempelhof).
- Most flights arrive at Tegel, to the north, and Schönefeld, in the east. Tempelhof, in the south, handles domestic and charter flights.
- Tegel (Flughafen Berlin-Tegel) 🚩 B1 ☎ 01805000186 for information (5AM–11:30PM) 🚌 109 to Ku'damm and Zoo Station (Bahnhof Zoo)
- Tempelhof (Flughafen Berlin-Tempelhof) 🚩 J9

☎ 69512288 🅤 U-Bahn line 6 (Platz der Luftbrücke *not* Tempelhof). Change at Friedrichstrasse for the west end 🚌 119 for Ku'damm
- Schönefeld (Flughafen Berlin-Schönefeld) 🚩 Off map to southeast ☎ 60910 🅢 S-Bahn line 9 to Zoo Station via Alexanderplatz

Arriving by bus

- All long-distance coaches arrive at the central bus station at the Funkturm in Messedamm. Travel information ☎ 3018028

Arriving by train

- Good connections from Paris, Brussels, Copenhagen, Warsaw, Moscow, Vienna and Prague.
- The main stations are Berlin-Lichtenberg and Zoo Station (Bahnhof Zoo).
- Train information: Deutsche Bahn AG (German National Railway) 🚩 E6 ✉ Hardenbergstrasse 20 ☎ 19419 For train information ☎ 01805996633

Travelling by car

- A ring road provides access from north and south.
- Visitors can telephone a Mitfahrzentrale (ride centre) to arrange a lift to other German cities in a private car (rates to be agreed beforehand). Mitfahrzentralen are located at: Liebland, U-Bahn Zoo, platform 2 🚩 E6 ☎ 19440 (daily 9AM–8PM) U-Bahn Alexanderplatz 🚩 K5 ☎ 2415820 (Mon–Fri 9AM–8PM; Sat 10–6; Sun 11–4) U- or S-Bahn Yorckstrasse 🚩 H8 ☎ 2164020 (Mon–Fri 9AM–8PM; Sat–Sun 10–6)

Customs regulations

- No currency restrictions.
- Duty-free limits for non-EU visitors are: 200 cigarettes or 250g of tobacco or 50 cigars; 2 litres of wine and 1 litre of spirits.

ESSENTIAL FACTS

Electricity
- 220 volts on a two-pin plug.

Etiquette
- It is polite to say *Guten Tag* (good day) and *Auf Wiedersehen* (goodbye) when shopping and *Entschuldigen Sie* (excuse me) in crowds.
- Never jaywalk or jump lights at pedestrian crossings.
- Informal dress is the norm when dining out in Berlin. However, nightclubs are dressier while the theatre and opera are more formal.

Money matters
- On 1 January 1999 the Euro became the official currency of Germany. Euro notes and coins were introduced on 1 January 2002. The German Deutschmark (DM) will be removed from circulation by early 2002.
- Exchange offices (*Wechselstuben*) can be found all over Berlin: Zoo Station (Bahnhof Zoo) 🕇 E6 🕓 Mon–Sat 7:30AM–10PM; Sun and holidays 8–7 Friedrichstrasse station 🕇 J5 🕓 Mon–Fri 7AM–7:30PM; Sat–Sun 8–4; holidays 9–2
- Automatic cash dispensers (ATMs) can be found citywide.
- Most major credit cards (American Express, MasterCard, Visa, EuroCard and Diners Club) are recognised but not widely accepted.
- Euro traveller's cheques are preferred, but those in major European currencies and US dollars are acceptable.
- American Express Offices: 🕇 E7 ✉ Uhlandstrasse 173–4 ☎ 8827575 🕇 J5 ✉ Friedrichstrasse 172 ☎ 20455721

Opening hours
- Shops 🕓 Mon–Fri 9:30–6:30; Sat 9–2. On Thursdays some shops stay open till 8PM
- Banks 🕓 Mon–Fri 9–12:30. Afternoons vary
- Pharmacies 🕓 Mon–Fri 9:30–6:30; Sat 9–2 ☎ 01141 for night pharmacies

Places of worship
- Religious services information: ☎ 01157
- Protestant: Kaiser Wilhelm Memorial Church (►34) ☎ 2185023. Services 🕓 Sun 10AM, 6PM (9AM in English during summer)
- Berliner Dom (►45) ☎ 20269111. Services 🕓 Sun 10AM, 6PM (Evensong in English Thu 6PM)
- Roman Catholic: Hedwigskirche (►43) ☎ 2034810. Masses 🕓 Sun 8AM, 10AM, noon, 6PM; Sat 7PM
- Anglican: St. George's 🕇 Off map to west ✉ Preussenallee. Holy Communion 🕓 Sun 8AM. Morning service 🕓 10AM
- Conservative Jewish: Synagogue Pestalozzistrasse 🕇 D6 ✉ Pestalozzistrasse 14 ☎ 3138411. Services 🕓 Fri 6PM; Sat 9:30AM
- Orthodox Jewish: Adass Jisroel 🕇 J4 ✉ Tucholsky Strasse 40. Services 🕓 Fri 5PM; Sat 9:30AM

Public holidays
- 1 January; Good Friday; Easter Monday; 1 May; Ascension Day; Pentecost Monday; 3 October (German Unity Day); Christmas Day; 26 December.

Student travellers
- Special fares from Deutsche Bahn for young people with a *Reisepasse*.
- Discounts of up to 50 per cent on public transport, in museums and in some theatres are available on production of an International Student Identity Card.
- European 'Transalpino' tickets are also available for people under 26.

Time differences
- Berlin is six hours ahead of Eastern Standard Time in winter and two hours ahead in summer.

Tipping
- A service charge is usually included in hotel and restaurant bills. Tip porters, maids and washroom attendants.

Toilets
- Men's toilets are labelled *Herren*, women's *Damen* or *Frauen*.
- Public toilets are free but scarce. Use those in cafés, restaurants, hotels and department stores.

Travel Insurance
- Take out full health and travel insurance before travelling to Germany.

Women travellers
- Schokofabrik (Women's Centre):
  🛇 L7 ✉ Marianenstrasse 6
  ☎ 6152440 🕓 Café: Mon–Fri 1PM–midnight; Sun noon–2PM. Turkish bath: Sun–Fri 11–10

PUBLIC TRANSPORT

- Berlin has an excellent public transport network, with two urban railways and numerous bus and tram routes. The local transport authority is the Berliner Verkehrs-Betriebe (BVG).
- Information: BVG-Pavillon 🛇 E6
  ✉ Hardenbergplatz (Zoo Station) ☎ 29712971
  travel information ☎ 19449 customer services
  🕓 Daily 6AM–11PM
- BVG lost property: BVG Tempelhof 🛇 Off map to south
  ✉ Lorenzweg 5 ☎ 25623040

Types of ticket
- The **24-hour ticket** (*Tageskarte*) and the weekly **7-*Tageskarte*** allow unlimited travel on the entire BVG network (trains, buses, trams and the ferry from Wannsee to Kladow). The weekly ticket covers unlimited travel during any seven-day period from validation until midnight on the seventh day.
- A **single ticket** is valid for two hours. You can transfer or interrupt your travel.
- The *Kurzstrecke* (short-distance ticket) is valid on the U- and S-Bahn for up to three stops including transfers, or for six stops only (bus/tram).
- The *Sammelkarte* (multiple ticket) must be stamped before each ride in the red ticket machines on buses and at station entrances.
- **BerlinWelcomeCard** entitles one adult and up to three children aged 6–14 to free BVG travel for three days as well as reductions on sightseeing trips, museums, theatres and other attractions. Enquire at your hotel, tourist information offices or U-Bahn ticket offices.
- Children under 14: reduced-rate travel; children under six: free.

The metro
- The U-Bahn (underground railway) and S-Bahn (city railway) are complementary and interchangeable.
- You must first buy a valid ticket from station foyers or from vending machines on platforms. Routes are referred to by the final stop on the line.
- You must validate your ticket at a machine on the platform before boarding the train.
- Trains run every five or ten minutes, Mon–Fri 4AM–midnight; Sat–Sun (approximately)

4AM–2AM. On Friday and Saturday, trains on U-Bahn lines 9 and 12 run throughout the night at 15-minute intervals. Most S-Bahn trains operate until 4AM.

- You may take bicycles on the U-Bahn on weekdays between 9AM and 2PM and after 5:30PM, and all weekend. Cyclists may travel on the S-Bahn at any time. There is a small charge.

Buses

- Central Bus Station, Funkturm ☎ 3018028
- Enter the cream-coloured double-deckers at the front and leave by the doors in the middle or at the back. Pay the driver with small change or show ticket (see above). Multiple tickets, also valid for U- and S-Bahn, can be bought from vending machines at some bus stops or at U-Bahn stations, but not from the driver.
- Route 100 is particularly useful, departing from Zoo Station every 10 minutes and linking the West End with Unter den Linden and Alexanderplatz.
- More than 70 night buses operate half-hourly from 1AM to 4AM. Line N19 runs through the centre every 15 minutes.
- Buses have rear-door access and safety straps for wheelchairs.
- Wheelchair users may find the Telebus service useful: Telebus-Zentrale ✚ E7 ✉ Joachimstaler Strasse 17 ☎ 4775440

Strassenbahnen

- Trams operate largely in eastern Berlin. Ticket procedures are the same as for buses.

Maps and timetables

- Obtain timetables and maps from the BVG-Pavillon (▶ 90) and from U-Bahn station ticket offices. Tourist Information Offices also have transport information.

Taxis

- Taxis are good value, with stands throughout the city. Use only cabs with a meter.
- There is a small surcharge for baggage.
- Not all drivers know their way, so travel with your own map and be able to pinpoint your destination.
- Contact numbers ☎ 69022, 261026, 210101, 443322
- Chauffeur service ☎ 2139090
- Bike taxis (rickshaws) ☎ 44358990

BVG ferries

- BVG ferry lines in the Wannsee and Köpenick areas include services from Wannsee to Kladow, Glienicker Bridge to Sacrow, Grünau to Wendenschloss and around Müggelsee.

MEDIA & COMMUNICATIONS

Telephones

- In phone boxes marked *Kartentelefon* use phone cards, available from post offices, petrol stations and newspaper kiosks.
- Boxes marked *International* and telephones in post offices are for long-distance calls.
- Calls are cheapest after 10PM and on Sundays.
- Follow the dialling instructions (in several languages) in the box.
- The country code for Germany is 0049.
- The area code for Berlin (from outside the city) is 030.
- To call the UK from Berlin dial 0044.

- To call Berlin from the UK dial 0049 30 (then the number).
- For information dial 01188.
- Local operator 03, international 0010.

Post offices

- Open: 🕐 Mon–Fri 8–6; Sat 8–noon
- Poste restante (*postlagernd*): use the post office at Joachimsthaler Strasse 7 🕐 Mon–Sat 8AM–midnight; Sun 10AM–midnight ☎ 018023333
- US citizens can receive mail at the American Express Office ✉ Ku'damm 11 ☎ 8827575
- Other post offices: ✉ Alte Potsdamer Strasse 7 🕐 Mon–Fri 9AM–8PM; Sat 9AM–4PM ✉ Nürnberger Strasse 8 🕐 Mon–Fri 8AM–6PM; Sat 8AM–1PM
- Stamps can be bought from vending machines on the Ku'damm as well as from post offices.
- Postboxes are bright yellow.

Newspapers and magazines

- National dailies published in Berlin include *Die Welt* and *Bild*.
- Local dailies include *Tagesspiegel*, *Tageszeitung*, *Berliner Morgenpost*, *Berliner Zeitung*, *Berliner Kurier*.
- Most large hotels and news-stands stock major European dailies and the *International Herald Tribune*.
- Useful listings magazines include *Tip, Zitty* (both twice monthly, in German); *Berlin TutGut* (from Tourist Information, in English); *Berlin Das Magazin* (quarterly, in English and German); *Berlin Programm* (monthly, in German).

Radio

- BBC World Service 90.2FM.

Television

- There are several German channels, such as ARD and ZDF, but the choice of satellite and cable channels is increasing. Major hotels provide CNN, Sky News and BBC world news broadcasts, an English-language sports channel and MTV.
- *Zitty* magazine lists programmes.

EMERGENCIES

Sensible precautions

- Although Berlin is one of the safer European cities, always remain on your guard.
- Avoid poorly lit areas, especially around Potsdamer Platz.
- Potsdamer Strasse is the centre of a seedy red-light district at night.
- Thieves often target tourists on the U-Bahn, so keep wallets and purses concealed.
- Bicycle theft is common, so if you hire a bike make sure you use the lock that is routinely provided.

Lost property

- Police, Tempelhof ➕ J9 ✉ Platz der Luftbrücke 6 ☎ 6995
- BVG Transport Lost and Found ☎ 25623040

Medical and dental treatment

- There are plenty of English-speaking doctors in Berlin. For a referral service telephone the medical emergency number.
- Emergency numbers:
  Medical ☎ 310031
  Dental ☎ 89004333
  Poison ☎ 19240

Medicines

- Take any specially prescribed medications with you.
- Pharmacy opening hours (➤ 89).

Emergency phone numbers

- Coins are not needed for

emergency calls from public
telephones:
Police ☎ 110
Fire ☎ 112
Ambulance ☎ 115
• American Hotline: crisis hotline
and free, recorded medical
referral service ☎ 0177 8141510

Embassies in Berlin
• UK ✉ Unter den Linden 32–4 ☎ 201840
• USA ✉ Neustädtischer Kirchstrasse 4–5
☎ 2385174

German National Tourist Office
• UK ✉ PO Box 2695, London W1A 3TN
☎ 020-7317 0908

Tourist information offices
• Verkehrsamt Berlin,
Europa-Center ✚ E6
✉ Budapester Strasse 45 🕓 Mon–Sat
8:30AM–8:30PM; Sun 10–6:30PM
• Airport Tegel 🕓 Daily 5AM–10:30PM
• KaDeWe Reisecenter
✉ Tauentzienstrasse 21–24 🕓 Mon–Fri
9:30AM–8PM; Sat 9AM–4PM
• Brandenburg Gate 🕓 Daily 9:30AM–6PM
• Berlin Tourismus Marketing
GmbH (office) ✉ Am Karlsbad 11
☎ 250025 (Hotline)

LANGUAGE

yes	ja
no	nein
please	bitte
thank you	danke
good morning	guten Morgen
good evening	guten Abend
good night	gute Nacht
goodbye	auf Wiedersehen
today	heute
yesterday	gestern
tomorrow	morgen
small	klein
large	gross
quickly	schnell

cold	kalt
hot	warm
good	gut
menu	die Speisekarte
breakfast	das Frühstück
lunch	das Mittagessen
dinner	das Abendessen
white wine	der Weisswein
red wine	der Rotwein
beer	das Bier
bread	das Brot
milk	die Milch
sugar	der Zucker
water	das Wasser
bill	die Rechnung
room	das Zimmer
open	offen
closed	geschlossen
how much?	wieviel?
expensive	teuer
cheap	billig
do you speak English?	sprechen Sie Englisch?
I don't speak German	Ich spreche kein Deutsch
I don't understand	Ich verstehe nicht
train station	der Bahnhof
airport	der Flughafen
bank	die Bank
post office	das Postamt
police	die Polizei
hospital	das Krankenhaus
Monday	Montag
Tuesday	Dienstag
Wednesday	Mittwoch
Thursday	Donnerstag
Friday	Freitag
Saturday	Samstag /Sonnabend
Sunday	Sonntag

one	eins	eleven	elf
two	zwei	twelve	zwölf
three	drei	thirteen	dreizehn
four	vier	fourteen	vierzehn
five	fünf	fifteen	fünfzehn
six	sechs	twenty	zwanzig
seven	sieben	twenty-one	
eight	acht		ein-und-zwanzig
nine	neun	fifty	fünfzig
ten	zehn	hundred	hundert

Index

A

accommodation 84–86
Ägyptisches Museum 50
airports 88
Alexanderplatz 47
Allied Forces Museum 50
Alliierten-Museum 50
Applied Art, Museum of 36, 48

B

Babelsberg Film Studio 15, 59
Bauhaus-Archiv 34
Bauhaus Museum 34
Berggruen Collection 52
Berlin Cathedral 45
Berliner Dom 45
Berlin Wall 12, 40
Berliner Schloss 45
Berliners 7, 9
Bernau 20
boat tours 19
Bode-Museum 43
Botanical Garden 56
Botanischer Garten 56
Brandenburg 21
Brandenburg Gate 39
Brandenburger Tor 39
Brecht-Haus 60
Breitscheidplatz 33
Britzer Garten 56
Bröhan Museum 50
Brücke Museum 52
buses and trams 88, 91

C

cabaret 79
Cecilienhof, Schloss 25
Charlottenburg, Schloss 31, 74
Checkpoint Charlie 7, 40
City Hall 47
city tours 19
climate 88
credit cards 89
crime 92
currency 89
customs regulations 88
cycling 60, 83, 92

D

Deutsche Staatsoper 42, 78
Deutscher Dom 41
Deutsches Historisches Museum 42

Deutsches Technikmuseum 51, 59
driving 88

E

Eastside Gallery 52
Egyptian Museum 50
electricity 89
Elisabethkirche 16
embassies 93
emergencies 92–93
Ephraimpalais 46
Ethnological Museum 30
Ethnologisches Museum 30
etiquette 89
Europa-Center 77
events 22, 82
excursions 19, 20–21

F

Fernsehturm 47
ferry services 91
Filmmuseum Berlin 51
folk, jazz and rock 82
food and drink
    bars 80–81
    cafés 32, 68–69
    eating out 62–69
    food shops 75
Französischer Dom 41
Freizeitpark Tegel 56
Friedrichs-Brücke 54
Friedrichwerdersche Kirche 53
Funkturm 57

G

galleries, commercial 73
Gedenkstätte Deutscher Widerstand 60
Gedenkstätte Haus der Wannsee Konferenz 55
Gemäldegalerie 35
Gendarmenmarkt 41
German History Museum 42
German Resistance, Memorial to 60
German Technology Museum 51, 59
Gertraudenbrücke 54
Gethsemane Kirche 53
Glienicker Brücke 26
Globe Fountain 33

'Gold Else' 37
Grips-Theater 59
Grunewald 28
Grunewaldsee 28
Grunewaldturm 28

H

Hedwigskirche 42
history 10–11
Hitler, Adolf 6, 12, 17, 60
hotels 84–86
Huguenot Museum 41
Humboldt University 42
hunting museum 28

I

Iduna House 32
immunisation 88
Indian & East Asian Art, Museums of 51
itineraries 14-15

J

Jagdschloss Grunewald 28
Jewish Museum 51
Jüdisches Museum 51
Jungfernbrücke 54

K

Kaiser-Wilhelm-Gedächtniskirche 33
Kaiser Wilhelm Memorial Church 33
Käthe Kollwitz memorial 16
Käthe-Kollwitz-Museum 32
Klein-Glienicke, Schloss 26
Kleistgrab 58
Kleistpark 17
Kleist's Grave 58
Klosterhof 26
Knoblauchhaus 46
Königliche Porzellan Manufaktor (KPM) 74
Konzerthaus 41
Köpenick, Schloss 48
Kreuzberg 18
Kronprinzenpalais 42
Krumme Lanke 28
Kulturforum 35
Kunstgewerbemuseum 36, 48
Kupferstich-Kabinett 52
Kurfürstendamm 32

L

Langes Luch 28
language 93
Lessingbrücke 54
Literaturhaus 32
lost property 92
Lübbenau 20-21
Lustgarten 45
Lutherhaus 20
Lutherstadt
  Wittenberg 20
Luxemburg, Rosa 37, 54

M

Marienkirche 47
markets 75
Marmorpalais 25
Martin-Gropius-Bau 52
Marx and Engels
  (sculptures) 58
Matschinsky-Denninghof
  sculpture 58
medical treatment 92
medicines 92
metro 90-91
Moabiter Brücke 54
Moltkebrücke 54
Monbijou Park 59
money 89
'Mont Klamott' 57
Moore, Henry
  (sculpture) 58
Müggelturm 57
Museum für Indische
  Kunst; Ostasiatische
  Kunst 51
Museumsinsel 43
Museums Island 43
Musical Instruments,
  Museum of 35

N

Napoleon 12
Neue Nationalgalerie 35
Neue Synagoge 51, 53
Neue Wache 42
New National Gallery 35
New Palace 24
New Synagogue 51, 53
newspapers and
  magazines 92
nightclubs 80-81
Nikolaikirche 46
Nikolaiviertel 46

O

Oberbaumbrücke 54

Old Royal Library 42
Olympiastadion 57, 83
Olympic Stadium 57, 83
opening hours 89

P

Pariser Platz 39
Park Babelsberg 57
passports and visas 88
Peacock Island 59
Pergamon Museum 44
Pfaueninsel 59
pharmacies 89
places of worship 53, 89
population 8
post offices 92
Potsdam Conference 25
Potsdam Film Museum 15
Potsdamer Platz 6, 7
Prenzlauer Berg 16
Prinz-Albrecht-Palais 38
public holidays 89
public transport 90-91

Q

Quadriga 39

R

radio and television 92
Rathaus Schöneberg
  17, 55
Regierungsviertel 6, 38
Reichstag 55
Rotes Rathaus 47

S

Sachsenhausen 29
Sanssouci, Schloss 24
Savignyplatz 18
Scheunenviertel 16
Schinkel, K. F. 26, 31, 39,
  41, 42, 53, 54, 56
Schleusenbrücke 54
Schloss Glienicke 26
Schlossbrücke 54
Schlossinsel 48
Schöneberg 17
sensible precautions 92
shopping 70-77, 89
Siegessäule 37
Sophienkirche 53
Soviet War Memorial 58
Sowjetisches Ehrenmal 58
Spandau Zitadelle 27
sport 83
Spreewald 20
Story of Berlin 51

student travellers 89

T

taxis 91
telephone numbers,
  emergency 92-93
telephones 91-92
Teufelsberg 28
theatres and concerts 78
Tiergarten 6, 7, 37
Tierpark Berlin-
  Friedrichsfelde 56
time differences 90
toilets 90
Topographie des Terrors
  38
Topography of Terror 38
tourist offices 93
train services 88, 90-91
traveller's cheques 89
travelling to Berlin 88
Treptower Park 56

U

Unter den Linden 42

V

Viktoriapark 56
Villa Grisebach 32
Volkspark
  Jungfernheide 56

W

walks 16-18, 19
Wannsee Conference
  Centre 55
Wannsee-Kladow ferry
  60
Wars of Liberation,
  Monument to the 56
Wilhelm II, Kaiser 12, 25,
  28, 33
Winterfeldtplatz 17, 75
Wittenbergplatz
  U-Bahn 60
women travellers 90

Z

Zeiss-Grossplanetarium
  59
Zeughaus 42
Zille 58
Zitadelle 27
Zoo and Aquarium 59
Zoologischer Garten 59
Zum Nussbaum 46, 69

CityPack
Berlin

Written by Christopher and Melanie Rice
Edited, designed and produced by
AA Publishing
Maps © Automobile Association Developments Limited 1996, 1999, 2002
Fold-out map © RV Reise- und Verkehrsverlag Munich · Stuttgart
© Cartography: GeoData

Distributed in the United Kingdom by AA Publishing, Millstream, Maidenhead Road, Windsor, Berkshire, SL4 5GD.

The contents of this publication are believed correct at the time of printing. Nevertheless, the publishers cannot be held responsible for any errors or omissions or for changes in the details given in this guide or for the consequences of any reliance on the information provided by the same. Assessments of attractions, hotels, restaurants and so forth are based upon the author's own personal experience and, therefore, descriptions given in this guide necessarily contain an element of subjective opinion which may not reflect the publishers' opinion or dictate a reader's own experiences on another occasion.

We have tried to ensure accuracy in this guide, but things do change and we would be grateful if readers would advise us of any inaccuracies they may encounter.

Published by AA Publishing (a trading name of Automobile Association Developments Limited, whose registered office is Millstream, Maidenhead Road, Windsor, Berkshire, SL4 5GD. Registered number 1878835).

Colour separation by Daylight Colour Art Pte Ltd, Singapore
Printed and bound by Dai Nippon Printing Co (Hong Kong) Ltd.

ACKNOWLEDGEMENTS
The Automobile Association would like to thank the following photographers, libraries and associations for their assistance in the preparation of this book. Bauhaus-Archiv, Berlin (Gunteer Lepowski) 49b; James Davis Worldwide F/Cover, bandsman; Rex Features Ltd 9; Spectrum Colour Library F/Cover, Brandenburg Gate; World Pictures 40.
All remaining pictures are held in the Association's own library (AA PHOTO LIBRARY) and were taken by CLIVE SAWYER, with the exception of pages 17, 32, 48a, 48b, 51, 55, 57, which were taken by A BAKER; pages 1, 2, 5a, 5b, 13a, 13b, 23, 28, 30a, 30b, 31a, 31b, 33a, 33b, 34, 36b, 37a, 37b, 39a, 41b, 43, 44, 45b, 47a, 50, 53, 56, 59, 60, 61a, 61b, 87a, 87b, which were taken by A SOUTER; and pages 49a, taken by D TRAVERSO.

The authors are grateful to the following for assistance in the updating of this book:
AB Airlines, Gabriella Schiller (Berlin Philharmonic Orchestra), Natascha Kompatzki and Dr Buri (Berlin Tourismus Marketing).

REVISION VERIFIERS *Christopher and Melanie Rice*
ORIGINAL COPY-EDITOR *Julia Brittain* INDEXER *Marie Lorimer*

TITLES IN THE CITYPACK SERIES
• Amsterdam • Bangkok • Barcelona • Beijing • Berlin • Boston •
• Brussels & Bruges • Chicago • Dublin • Florence • Hong Kong • Lisbon •
• London • Los Angeles • Madrid • Melbourne • Miami • Montréal • Munich •
• New York • Paris • Prague • Rome • San Francisco • Seattle • Shanghai •
• Singapore • Sydney • Tokyo • Toronto • Venice • Vienna • Washington •